D0581733

GUIDE
TO
MEDITATION

GUIDE
TO
MEDITATION

Caroline Tosh

CAXTON REFERENCE

© 2001 Caxton Editions

This edition published 2001 by Caxton Publishing Group Ltd,
20 Bloomsbury Street, London, WC1B 3QA.

Design and compilation by The Partnership Publishing Solutions Ltd,
Glasgow, G77 5UN

Printed and bound in India

CONTENTS

CHAPTER 1
Introduction

The practice of meditation originated in the East thousands of years ago but has become rapidly accepted in the West in recent years. As our society expands at an ever-accelerating pace, conventional medicine can no longer supply a panacea for every ailment. People are now looking to more alternative forms of therapy and are beginning to realise that in order to feel an all-over sense of well being it is necessary to consider their health from a holistic point of view. Furthermore, as society becomes increasingly material, many people feel the urge to transcend the desire to accumulate possessions and advance their social status, choosing instead to explore their own potential as individuals and to achieve a sense of inner contentment that material success does not bring.

In the West there are many forms of meditation being practised. These include Indian Yoga, Buddhism, Tibetan Buddhism, Zen Buddhism and perhaps the most popular form, Transcendental Meditation. There are two main reasons for practising meditation. The first is that meditation is seen as a means of counteracting the stress created by the hectic pace of our everyday lives, and allows us to truly relax. This provides both mental and physical relief. Mediation can therefore be seen as an effective method of combating physical illness such as high blood pressure, lethargy and anxiety. Secondly, while meditation holds the key to physical and mental health, it can also add a spiritual dimension to our lives. In the West, we are obsessed with obtaining success in many different ways, such as furthering our advancement up the career ladder, acquiring material possessions, enjoying an active social life, building relationships with others. It is natural that we strive to achieve these goals and there is nothing intrinsically wrong with them, but it . means that our happiness is entirely dependent on external transitory factors. The achievement of these goals does bring satisfaction and happiness but this will not last indefinitely and it will not solve any of our problems. Most things, including our job, our friends, our possessions, will at some point leave us and if we are too dependent on them then we can be left with very little substance in our lives when they do. With meditation, we can find lasting contentment in an increased awareness of ourselves and while we can still enjoy the same things, they are simply an extra pleasure rather than the sole cause of our happiness. This increased spirituality means we are happier, more contented people which can also improve our relationships with others.

While meditation is becoming increasingly popular,

some people are inevitably put off by the overly mystical image that surrounds it. This has much to do with more traditional Eastern approaches to mediation where it is practised as a form of worship, and it is common for novices to be guided by an already enlightened teacher or guru. There is also a common misperception that meditation is a tedious discipline where one must empty the mind of all thoughts whilst contorting the body into various uncomfortable positions. When you begin to meditate, you may find that friends or partners are sceptical or even disapproving about it. It can be human nature to mock things that we know very little about and therefore you should not worry too much about this reaction. They are probably even a little envious that you have the courage to try something new.

The interest in meditation in the West is less motivated by a desire to convert to a particular religion and more to with reaping the spiritual and physical benefits which it brings. Meditation in its basic form does not adhere to any one religion. In fact, it manages to embody the main principles of most major religions as it promotes self-awareness therefore enhancing tolerance towards and relationships with others. It combines the promotion of love and compassion with a relaxed state of mind, thus rendering the individual more receptive to new ways of thinking. If you are already religious, it can strengthen your faith or allow you to become clearer on what your beliefs actually are. When you reach a state of contentment with yourself and other people, this can only be a good thing, and if everyone shared that contentment then our society would no doubt be a more tolerant and peaceful one.

As there exists many different religions in the West and as some individuals prefer not to adhere to any one religion, it is perhaps more useful to take the basic concepts behind meditation and adapt them to suit the Western lifestyle. Meditation should be a flexible discipline that can be adapted to suit the particular problems and needs of the individual who is practising it. It allows us to explore the contents of the mind and enter the unconscious, thus discovering more about ourselves and about life in general.

Many people that meditation is beneficial as it manages to slow down their thought processes. Our minds are constantly active and are saturated with new ideas, sensory impressions and unconscious drives and desires. It is busy both day and night and never shuts down. Even when we are asleep, our thoughts may slow down but our minds are still working. This slowing down of the mind during sleep is essential to allow us to absorb our thoughts and arrange them into some sort of order. Like meditation, it is an excellent way of relieving stress and it allows us to step back from the hectic pace of daily life, but we are not conscious during sleep and often forget what our thoughts were once we have woken up.

Meditation is more beneficial than sleep precisely because we are in a similar relaxed state, but we are conscious and can guide our thoughts. We can also hold onto the relaxed feeling and higher consciousness which meditation brings and, on finishing the meditation, we can also try to apply this to our everyday lives, as we do not forget our thoughts as we do with sleep. Meditation also allows us to calm the mind in a way that we cannot do during sleep. This deep state of relaxation while remaining alert is what provides a release for the physical and mental stress that accumulates from day to day. Meditation provides a more long-term and effective solution for dealing with stress than reliance of substances of any kind, and it is also far less harmful to the body.

The clarity of thought of thought that meditation brings improves our sense of emotional well being while enhancing our efficiency and ability to cope in everyday life. Many people who practise meditation have reported that since they have started meditation regularly, they are able to deal with situations that would previously have sent them into a panic. Many people who have religious beliefs also find that they feel a connection with some higher level of consciousness, something that cannot be ruled out as being possible even for those who have no definite beliefs.

Stress is one of the most widespread medical conditions throughout society in the 21st century. It can also cause us to become more susceptible to other illnesses, both mental and physical. Dissipating stress is the only way we will truly achieve happiness and contentment in life. Stress is caused by a combination of factors. Every day we will encounter situation which challenge us. If we approach these tasks with a positive attitude and are realistic about our abilities, then we will not suffer from high levels of stress. However, if we doubt our abilities due to deep-seated feelings of inadequacy or low self-esteem, or if we strive to achieve more than is realistically possible then we shall become overwhelmed. This is when we encounter stress.

Meditation is said to be one of the most effective methods of combating stress available. Meditation puts us in touch with our inner self. Through meditation we come to know ourselves better and this allows us to be realistic about our own abilities, putting an end to those irrational overreactions which cause stress levels to increase. Thus, meditation does not only relieve stress but can prevent it from accumulating to such a degree in the first place.

Once you begin to act upon this stress, you will become aware of a huge difference to your life. You will feel more energetic, more enthusiastic and more able to cope with situations that you would previously have been daunted by. This increased feeling of buoyancy will not go unnoticed by others. You will emanate a sense of positivity that others will be attracted to and feel comfortable in the presence of. You will also feel more tolerance and warm feeling towards others, something that can only enhance your relationships, both in the workplace and in the home.

While meditation is considered by many as being one of the most effective ways to beat stress, there are many other alternative therapies you might want to use to supplement your meditation practice. In a later chapter, we will consider the practises of yoga, and the Alexander Technique, which of all other alternative health therapies seem to complement meditation particularly well. These practises are also considered to be highly effective when relieving stress and, what is more, provide an excellent way of priming your body before meditating and of improving your performance during the meditation itself.

While meditation and other natural therapies probably supply the most effective method of stress-reduction, most people when suffering from stress are likely to feel that they do not have the time to take up such things. The most common reactions to stress is either to visit the doctor and request some form of prescription drug, or to rely heavily on cigarettes, alcohol, or other substances to help keep the stressful feelings at bay. While these substances may appear to relieve stress in the short-term, they are not doing you or your body much good at all. While you take them they merely mask the unpleasant feelings you are suffering from without looking at the source of them or ridding you of them on a permanent basis. They alter your perception, imbuing you with a temporary sense of well being. However, this is only temporary and when the effect starts to wear off the body suffers withdrawal symptoms from the drug and you will often feel lower than you were before. Meditation provides only the sense of well being without any comedown afterwards and its benefit should remain long after you have finished meditating. Furthermore, it is free of charge and can do you no physical harm.

Many people are even unaware that they are suffering from stress and it has become an almost acceptable condition to be suffering from in our society. People tend to associate high levels of stress with those who work in high-powered jobs but it is not only limited to such people. For example, someone who is unemployed can be suffering more stress than a high-powered business-woman is suffering simply because they feel a sense of failure and underachievement. The businesswoman may enjoy the adrenaline rush that her hectic lifestyle brings and be suffering only minimal levels of stress. It is not just our lifestyles that determine the level of stress that we will suffer, but our perception of our lifestyles along with our often-fallacious perception of our ability to cope.

Meditation can not only help to relieve stress but can improve your life in other ways, too. It can help to broaden your mind and increase your confidence in your own abilities. Once you begin meditating on a regular basis, you will probably find that you will start to examine your old lifestyle with a critical eye and will want to make changes. This is an entirely positive thing and you should think of it as an opportunity for a mental spring-cleaning session, where you rid yourself of all those old habits that you no longer need to make way for a new set of ideas and a new way of life.

Meditation can also enhance creativity. Meditation frees our thinking from set and unproductive patterns of thought. When meditating, it is likely that you will find that all sorts of new ideas will flood into your mind. It is always a good idea to keep a pen and pad next to you when meditating so that when you finish the meditation you can jot down these ideas before you forget them as you may want to explore them further once your meditation is over. As meditation broadens the mind and allows us to get to know ourselves more intimately, it is also possible that you may discover new talents or interests. Feel free to experiment with whatever awakens your interest. Things like painting and music are particularly good as they allow us to explore our own feeling and express ourselves further.

So meditation can be used to eliminate stress and help you understand your unconscious fears and desires so that you can understand our behaviour patterns and change them if necessary. With lower levers of stress, you will be a happier more contented person and more able to deal with both the minor and major problems that life holds for us all. You will be more freethinking, more creative and more approachable to other people.

Most importantly, meditation should be an enjoyable activity. It should not feel like a chore or you will find it hard to fully let go and reap the benefits from it and may even be tempted to give it up before it has had a chance to do you any good. The feeling of relaxation gleaned from a meditation should be something to look forward to in the way that you would look forward to a warm bath after a long and tiring day. You should look forward to your meditation as a time in which you can be entirely alone, where you can transcend the stresses of daily life and become completely immersed in your own thoughts.

Meditation is often sought as a refuge from the world, but you will emerge from each session like a butterfly from a cocoon – revitalised and re-energised – in short, a new person.

In this book, we will look at meditation as the tool to promote growth and development. This means both physical improvement – i.e. controlling stress and boosting a sense of well being – and spiritual growth. Used effectively, meditation can help people overcome addictions, become more efficient in day-to-day living and become more rounded and fulfilled individuals.

In order to understand meditation, it is necessary to first identify what 'the mind', or 'consciousness', is. There are many different types of meditation but they all attempt to achieve a similar objective, which is to improve the quality of our life by relaxing the body and understanding the workings of the mind.

When we meditate, we attempt to transcend the stress of our daily life and achieve a more lucid and complete awareness of existence as it really is. In the old days, it was believed that people were composed of a body and a soul, and that the mind and body were not considered to be two separate entities. The notion continued until the c17th French philosopher, Descartes, proposed the notion that body and soul were, in fact, quite separate entities while being interdependent. It is difficult for us to fully comprehend the mind due to the limitations of the mind itself, but it is generally accepted that it is composed of a conscious part and an unconscious part. The conscious part of the mind perceives reality and makes choices based on those perceptions, and the unconscious part stores our memories and is the source of many of our drives and desires, usually without our even being aware of it. Meditation allows us to tap into both the conscious and the unconscious parts of the mind.

In the previous chapter we have touched some of the potential benefits of practising meditation, but what exactly is it, and what does it involve? *The Oxford English Dictionary* (1995) gives the following definition:

Meditate: *v* **1. a.** *Intr.* Exercise the mind in (especially religious) contemplation. **b.** (Usually followed by on, upon) focus on a subject in this manner. **2.** *tr.* Plan mentally; design.

The dictionary gives a broad definition and also shows how common it is to perceive meditation as a religion ritual of some kind. The working definition we shall use in this book is that meditation is a combination of a deep state of relaxation and a heightened consciousness or awareness. The combination of these two states is uncommon. In an extreme state of relaxation we tend to be less mentally alert, for example when we are asleep. And when our minds are particularly aroused, during sports, for example, our bodies tend to be active, too. While the development of the mind is the main goal of meditation, a relaxed body is necessary to facilitate this. The first step in learning to meditate is therefore learning to relax. This can be more difficult than it sounds, especially if you have a hectic, stressful lifestyle and are not in the habit of relaxing properly. It can be hard to find the time and to completely relax mind and body but once mastered this can provide relief for stress and all the problems associated with it.

Physical Benefits

Stress originates through a placing too high a demand on oneself. We have to learn through enhanced self-awareness the limit of our own abilities and tailor our lifestyles to suit, rather than forcing ourselves to meet the demands enforced upon us by our lifestyles. Stress is a common problem that can be seen as being symptomatic of our culture, and many people do not even realise that they are suffering from it. Signs of stress include insomnia, high blood pressure, the formation of poor relationships, irritability and even depression. Stress can create a difficult cycle to break as these symptoms combine to create a general feeling of malaise, thus increasing feelings of stress even more.

Meditation is an ideal method of combating stress. It will not remove the source of stress – this will have to be dealt with separately – but it can certainly help you become more aware of the factors in your life that need to be changed and it can give you the resolve necessary to change them. The relaxation involves in meditation will temporarily remove feelings of stress and tension but to remove them one more long-term basis, you will need to identify exactly what factors in your life are combining to cause these feelings and then work towards eliminating them one by one. These factors can be varied – they may include pressures at work, dysfunctional relationships, or even a poor diet. Whatever they may be, mediation can help you convert stress into a positive force and help you to turn your life around.

One of the benefits of meditation is, contrary to what many people believe, you do not have to adopt any particular posture as long as you are comfortable and relaxed. Nor is it physically demanding. These aspects of meditation mean that anyone can practice it, even those people who have a disability or have a low level of fitness.

When meditating, you will realise just how much emphasis is placed on breathing correctly as by concentrating on your breathing patterns during a meditation is an ideal way of helping you focus on the mediation at hand. The physical benefits of breathing correctly are vast. Most people tend to take shallow, insubstantial breaths. Breathing more deeply than normal increases the supply of oxygen to the body whilst simultaneously ridding it of carbon dioxide. This, in turn, means that increased levels of oxygen will be absorbed into the bloodstream, which will be used to convert food into energy, thus promoting all bodily functions. A higher concentration of oxygen in the blood means that the organs require less blood to function. Therefore, your heart can work less hard, which means that your blood pressure will be lowered and relaxation will be increased further.

Mental Benefits

Once the body is relaxed, our attention can turn to the mind. When we relax, not only is our body affected but our mind is, too. Relaxing lowers the frequency of brainwaves to a similar rate as to when we are asleep. This is necessary to allow the body to repair itself.

Relaxing does not only have tangible, physical benefits on the mind but also spiritual ones. Meditation has been criticised for promoting self-absorption – the idea being that an individual exploring the contents of his or her mind leads to concern for the self whilst oblivious to the external world. This is common fallacy. While the enhanced awareness facilitated by the meditative process does increase our self-awareness, it also increases our awareness our physical surroundings. For example, this can help us to improve relations with others by highlighting where we have perhaps been intolerant of a friend or colleague. However, as with problems of stress, meditation can only bring the problems to our attention. It is up to us to change the behavioural patterns that cause the problem in the first place.

Once basic meditation has been mastered, it is possible to use other, more complex methods to increase our self-knowledge and bring about change in our lives. When we dream, our conscious and unconscious feelings and anxieties are conveyed to us by imagery. A similar method can also be used in meditation to allow us to explore our minds and possibly even tap into the unconscious. This is known as 'guided imagery' and will be explored in a later chapter.

CHAPTER 3
Why Meditate?

Meditation initially originated as a way of training in religion and in the East this remains the ultimate goal. However, as organised religion is on the decline in the Western world, this form of meditation is less relevant. Most westerners that take up meditation are more concerned with the physical and mental benefits, which it brings about primarily through the release of stress. The physical and mental relaxation and profound sense of refreshment, which it brings, have been supported by scientific studies, which have examined physiological changes, which occur in those who meditate frequently.

Physiological Changes in the Body
Much scientific research has been carried out to investigate palpable, physical changes that occur in the body as a result of meditation. It is generally accepted that the following changes occur:
- The heart rate decreases
- Breathing slows down

- The body consumes less oxygen – a sign that metabolism has changed
- Blood pressure is normal – even in those who normally suffer from high blood pressure
- Brain waves become slower

All of these physiological changes support the theory that meditation is an aid to physical relaxation.

Psychosomatic Benefits

People turn to mediation for many varied reasons but the most common reasons would appear to be both the desires to improve the self and to boost physical well being. The relaxation involved in meditating has a direct effect on the body. Controlled breathing and thinking can be hugely beneficial to the body improving heart rate, blood pressure and even the digestive system. The nervous system becomes stronger and the individual becomes more able to deal with situations that would normally induce stress or fear. This is done by replacing the adrenaline rush that accompanies stressful situations with a more relaxed response. Energy levels are boosted and the mind is able to function with greater clarity than before.

Stress is basically a feeling of pressure or tension. This can be physical, for example, in the form of taut muscles, or mental, for example, in the form of insomnia. Stress is generally caused when we place too many demands on ourselves and it can creep up without us even noticing. The more stressed we feel, the less likely we are to be able to deal with a potentially stressful situation and the more stressed we become. Stress is also believed to contribute to our chances of contracting illness from the common cold to more life-threatening conditions such as cancer.

There are further physiological benefits to meditating on a regular basis. As the need for sleep increases when the individual is suffering from stress, it decreases when he/she begins to meditate on a regular basis. Problems such as insomnia disappear, and sleep becomes more productive as the person awakes feeling more refreshed than normal. The release from stress is accompanied by an increased feeling of exuberance – something which prescription drugs such as anti-depressants try to emulate through artificial means. Finding a natural alternative to relieve stress and contribute to a feeling of well being is often the first step in overcoming addiction and ending abuse of substances such as alcohol, cigarettes and prescription drugs. These substances may provide initial relief but are not a long-term solution, as they do not look challenge the source of the problem in the way that meditation can.

It has been mentioned that many people believe fallaciously that one of the purposes of meditation is to empty the mind and escape the physical world. In fact, one of the main purposes of meditation is to explore the mind and our conscious and unconscious thoughts and desires. The thinking behind this is that increased self-awareness allows us to interact more effectively with our external environment. This side of meditation can be extremely beneficial. The best thing of all is that is completely free of charge to meditate and there is no risk of any side effects either. So there is no harm in attempting to relieve physical ailments with meditation before looking to other forms of medicine.

The improved clarity of the mind that meditation brings means that concentration becomes easier and tasks that previously would have been mentally draining now require far less effort. With increased self-knowledge comes increased self-acceptance, thus imbuing the individual with a more relaxed approach to life and therefore promoting successful relationships with others and replacing negative emotions such as insecurity and envy with love and compassion. When meditation originated this was perhaps less important as people tended to meditate in solitary conditions, but in the Western world, life moves at a faster pace and we have contact with many different people on a daily basis. Thus, to enhance our sense of love and compassion for these people can eliminate feelings of animosity and improve our relationships whether these are with acquaintances or with loved ones.

While many Buddhists adhere to devotional practices when meditating, it is by no means necessary to subscribe to any form of religion in order to meditate. You are free to continue with your own beliefs regarding life and the universe – people of any religious persuasion, or of none at all, may meditate successfully.

Spiritual Enhancement

In contemporary Western society, the decline of religion and the break up of traditional communities has meant that many people now exist in a spiritual vacuum. The mark of success would appear to be advancement in our careers, or the attainment of material wealth. The spiritual dimension has become a secondary consideration or, in some cases, neglected altogether. There is nothing to teach us how valuable our lives are or to furnish us with a raison d'être. Many people can continue quite happily in this situation, but not indefinitely. Jobs and possessions can be lost so, without an increased spiritual awareness, we can be left with nothing. The more adept we become at meditation, the more enlightened we become spiritually, thereby increasing our sense of purpose and also our sense of contentment.

This notion of 'spiritual enlightenment' will not appeal to everyone and there is nothing that says everyone who meditates must be actively concerned with pursuing this state of increased awareness. However, it is something that will inevitably arise along the way, so it is perhaps most useful to consider what the term 'spiritual' means to you, so that each individual can define it for his or herself.

It is believed that meditation is safe for most people

to learn without requiring the supervision of an expert. It is very difficult to do yourself any harm with meditation even if, for example, you are not doing the positions correctly. Moreover, if you are not meditating properly to begin with, the correct procedure will usually come with practise so it is not a waste of time. The only people who should perhaps seek out expert advice before taking up meditation are those who are suffering from mental illness such as schizophrenia, those who are suffering from Attention Deficit Disorder or a similar condition, or those who suffer from epilepsy or seizures. If you suffer from, or even suspect that you suffer from, any of these conditions then it is best to seek out expert advice before you begin to meditate. Meditation is said to be a highly effective treatment of disorders such as these but if you were to choose an unsuitable form of meditation, then it could just make your condition worse.

CHAPTER 4
Meditation and Religion

While this book is more concerned with the technique of meditation in general rather than in adhering to any particular religion, it can be rewarding to explore the origins of meditation in order to see how those very methods developed. Many of the themes that people meditate on today originated as religious philosophies thousands of years ago. It is also interesting to see how widespread meditation is and not just throughout Eastern religions, but throughout most major religions in the world. If you are uninterested in the origins of meditation and are only concerned with learning various techniques then feel free to skip this chapter.

Buddhism

Meditation is an important part of the Buddhist religion, and Buddhist meditation is one of the most popular forms of meditation practised today. If you look at any book of meditation, you are likely to find in it meditations on various aspects of Buddhist philosophy. Even if the origins of the meditation are not acknowledged, many meditations practised today are influenced by ancient Buddhist philosophies.

The name Buddha comes from the Sanskrit word meaning 'to know,' a name which reflects his perceived wisdom. Buddha was a mortal named Gautama Siddhartha who is now considered to have been a God by his followers. As Buddha lived so long ago (approximately 540 BC) it is hard to tell what knowledge we have surrounding his life is true and what is mythical. It is said that he was a Hindu prince, born near Kathmandu in Nepal. He was apparently spoiled by his father, who wanted him to know no suffering or pain. He was therefore forbidden to leave the palace grounds in which he lived, and was surrounded by beautiful scenery, luxurious possessions and entertainment, such as the thousands of dancing girls that were apparently acquired for him.

While Buddha himself is said to have denied possessing any supernatural powers, people have since claimed that he was in fact a god. There are many myths that have been created in order to support this belief that he was supernatural. One such myth claims that, like Jesus, Buddha, was the product of a miraculous immaculate conception. Buddha's mother is said to have dreamt that a white elephant entered her body – an event that resulted in her falling pregnant. It is then said that one day as she stopped to pick some flowers in the garden of the palace, she gave birth to Buddha. Although he had just been born, the baby Buddha stood up, took seven steps and then

proclaimed that he was the 'world honoured one.'
Angels then appeared who lifted him up in a golden
net and sprinkled him with holy water. Another myth
includes the claim that Buddha emerged from the belly
of the Hindu god, Vishnu – a myth that highlights the
connection between Buddhism and Hinduism.

Buddhism is said to have emerged when Buddha
eventually requested that he be taken outside of the
palace to see what life was like for ordinary citizens.
He saw scenes of hardship including an old lame man
and a corpse being carried to a grave. The shock of
seeing such scenes of suffering after only knowing the
pleasures of life made an impact on the young Buddha.
He began to contemplate the nature of existence and
questioned the possibility of ever experiencing
happiness. Then one day after witnessing a begging
monk on the streets, Buddha believed that he had
found the key to happiness, which he believed was to
forsake worldly possessions and emotions, such as
desire and greed. The philosophy that people should
not rely on material objects for satisfaction is still
present in Buddhism today and is the subject of many
meditations.

This moment of epiphany when Buddha believed
himself to have found the key to happiness led him to
follow in the footsteps of this begging monk, and when
he was 29 he left his family and the palace behind and
took to the streets. Leaving his finery with his
charioteer, he set off on a journey of self-discovery. He
studied the arts of meditation and yoga with Hindu

gurus for some time and then having failed to find the happiness he sought, he abandoned this and joined a group of travelling monks who had an extremely ascetic form of existence. He travelled through India wearing only rags, and went without food for days on end. During these travels, Buddha became very close to nature – this led to his belief that all life is precious and that all things, both animate and inanimate, are to be appreciated, as they were made by a divine creator.

This appreciation of all life forms also led to the formation of the central tenet of Buddhism that all life is sacred human should therefore exercise love and compassion towards all other forms of love nature. This emphasis on the importance of love is present in many religions, but in Buddhism, this universal love should be displayed to all of mankind – not just our friends and family but everyone.

Buddha believed that this love towards all would be made universally possible if each individual achieved a clearer view of the nature of existence, and that this clarity would come through long periods of meditation. The importance of appreciating the true nature of existence is an idea central to the Buddhist faith and is a subject often meditated upon by Buddhists. We will look at meditations on the true nature of existence and on feeling love and compassion towards everyone in chapter 11 on insight meditation.

Buddha is then said to have continued contemplating the meaning of life and he went to meditate for 49 days. He was then interrupted by an evil spirit named Mara. She told him that mortals would never be able to understand his beliefs solely through meditation. This made him decide that it would be necessary for him to construct a system of beliefs that could be taught to others so that they too could benefit from his wisdom. He then meditated for another 49 days during which time he constructed a system of beliefs by which to live which consisted of his four noble truths and his eightfold path to enlightenment.

Approximately 9% of the world's population are Buddhist (42% are Christian, 20% are Hindu and 28% are Muslim). Buddhism is akin to a philosophical model that outlines an ideal way of living, as Buddhists have no God-like figure or supernatural elements in their religion. Buddha is said to be very different to Jesus, as there is no belief that he will help us to save our souls. There is no equivalent to Heaven and Hell in Buddhism, therefore there is no promise of reward for good behaviour or punishment for bad behaviour in the afterlife.

Buddha is considered less of a figure to be worshipped and more of an example on how to live. We are told that Buddha managed to find enlightenment through his own effort, and Buddhists are expected to follow his example and seek enlightenment through their own efforts by meditating on and contemplating the philosophy of Buddhism and following its guidance. Buddhism can be seen as a more relaxed religion than, for example, Christianity.

There is no equivalent to the bible or single manuscript that provides instruction on how to live. With Buddhism, the emphasis is placed on how we live in the here and now, and less thought to any afterlife. Buddhism provides us with a guide to a moral way of life that can be achieved through moderating our emotions and following a pattern of rational, thoughtful behaviour. Buddhists are encouraged to reflect on their behaviour through meditation and then and use the knowledge they glean from this as a catalyst for spiritual growth and change. There is no evidence in Buddhism of any of the miracles and supernatural powers present in other religions and Buddhist beliefs are also incompatible with prejudice and despotic governments. People should be practise tolerance, love and compassion and life should be enjoyed in moderation.

Buddha believed that the world is a place filled with pain and suffering. He saw life as inevitably leading towards death. He believed that when a person dies, they become reincarnated, and the aim of Buddhism was to find a way of putting an end to these endless reincarnations. Buddha believed himself to have provided an end to this through his middle way – the way of knowledge. The middle way was constructed as a result of Buddha's years spent wandering the land. He decided during this time that life was full of pain and suffering and therefore not worth living. But he also learned from his early years at the palace that a life consisting wholly of pleasure does not lead to happiness either. The way he believed each person should live was the middle way. Following the middle way consisted of each individual forsaking their desire for pleasure and worldly goods – those things that Buddha saw as the principle cause of human suffering.

In following the middle way, the individual was expected to show tolerance to other religions and practise moderation in life – i.e. to not become excessively ascetic or excessively hedonistic. Buddhism teaches that we should strive to achieve enlightenment and to do this we must strive to follow the four noble truths, which are:

- The first truth (Dukkha) can be summarised as stating that suffering is found throughout life, from the time that we are born until the time that we die. It also states that everything in existence is impermanent and will therefore come to and end – a belief that contemplated particularly often during Buddhist meditation.

- The second truth (Tanha) can be summarised by saying that suffering stems from our desire itself. Desire rears its head in the form of negative human emotions such as ignorance hatred, greed and intolerance.

- The third truth (Nirodha) is the termination of desire. If desire ceases to exist, then that individual has achieved Nirvana. Nirvana is difficult to explain or to comprehend as it exists beyond earthly experience.

- The fourth truth is also known as the Buddha's way.
  It comprises of the eight-fold paths to Nirvana (the
  Buddhist equivalent of the Ten Commandments of
  Christianity) of which meditation can be seen to be
  the final step. These are as follows:

  1　Right knowledge: To accept the four noble
  truths.
  2　Right aspiration or thought.
  3　Right speech: avoidance of obscenity and
  words that demean others. Avoid gossip and
  lies.
  4　Right behaviour: do not steal, practise
  promiscuity, abuse alcohol, or commit murder.
  5　Right effort: the necessary willpower to do
  right actions.
  6　Right livelihood: carry out honest work, never
  cheat, steal or show laziness at work. Never
  prostitute yourself, sell drugs, alcohol, meats,
  arms, or take part in slavery.
  7　Right mindfulness: i.e. our life is and will be
  determined by our own thoughts.
  8　Right concentration: the practise of meditation
  and yoga.

Zen Buddhism

Zen Buddhism developed out of Buddhism and, as
with Buddhism, meditation is very important within
the Zen Buddhist religion. While it also encompasses
Buddhist beliefs and has the ultimate goals of achieving

enlightenment and then Nirvana, Zen Buddhism has no rituals or guidance that adherents can follow. The word Zen translated means meditation, and this is perhaps the most important part of Zen Buddhism. Zen Buddhists believe that truth cannot be found without the use of meditation. Zen shares with Buddhism the emphasis that nature should be appreciated. Adherents of Zen believe further that a vital spark of energy runs through all living things and connects them.

The main goal of Zen Buddhism is that followers must comprehend that enlightenment, or satori, can only be achieved in the present, that is in the life of the follower. Enlightenment will only be achieved when the follower renounces all of the things that our society teaches us to strive for, such as creature comforts, material wealth, social status and even our sense of personal identity. The truth can only be found by meditation, so it is useless to devote time to prayer and ritual as the truth is said to be within each one of us. Reaching this state of enlightenment is the only way that Zen Buddhists believe that they will find true happiness.

Although life in a monastery is most suitable for a Zen Buddhist, anyone can become one through regular meditation. There is said to be no point studying scripture or recounting prayers, as Zen can only be learned through practising it rather than studying any theory behind it. Zen Buddhists believe that we all have the potential to become enlightened but we must look to ourselves to achieve this. It is recommended that novices do acquire an instructor though to keep them on the right path, something that would be difficult, although not impossible, to acquire in the West. This is due to the fact that meditation sessions in Zen Buddhism often consist of question and answer sessions also referred to as koan sessions. During these sessions, the guru will direct certain questions to the student. The student will soon come to realise that these questions are impossible to answer, as they have no logical or rational answer. The point of this is that it conveys the Zen Buddhist belief that life itself has no meaning or answers to yield so to look for any answer is pointless. The only thing that can be considered to have any meaning is the present life that we are experiencing. Even death is a useless concept to understand, as we cannot experience it in the here and now. Zen Buddhists believe that if we cannot directly experience something in the present then it is useless to ever attempt to understand it.

If you wish to become a Zen Buddhist, it is necessary that you spend much time meditating which involves learning correct body positions and breathing techniques. You must also learn to concentrate on the here and now – the time that you are experiencing. There is no point dwelling on the past or worrying about what the future may bring. Meditating on a regular basis is said to imbue the novice with a strong sense of discipline throughout their physical and mental being.

Taoism

As with Buddhism and Zen Buddhism, meditation is also a major part of Taoism.

China does not have a dominant religion but Taoism, Confucianism and Buddhism are all intrinsic to Chinese culture. According to Taoists, the founder of Taoism was a man called Lao Tzu who is also said to have taught Confucius. There is very little information available on the life of Lao Tzu and of what information there is, it is uncertain as to how true this is. He is said to have been born in approximately 551 BC and he is said to have written the *Tao Te Ching* (pronounced dao de jing, and translated as *The Way and the Power of Life*). Lao Tzu is believed to have been a minor government official as well as a teacher although little more than this is known about his life. Through the Tao Te Ching, Lao Tzu placed emphasis on the need for followers to live in harmony with nature. In his eyes, Taoism was a highly accessible religion. All that one had to do was to learn to be content with one's life, meditate on Taoist philosophies, and peace and enlightenment would come from within each individual.

As with Buddha, many myths have been created to make up for the lack of knowledge we have surrounding Lao Tzu's life. For example, it is said that, like Buddha, his conception was the product of an immaculate conception. It is also said that he had a star for a father and that he remained within the body of his mother for a total of 82 years, which meant that when born he was already an old man. It is said he lived the life of an anchorite for many years before attempting to find followers within his native land. When he failed to do so, it is said that he left for Tibet on the back of a buffalo.

Legend has it that when Lao Tzu attempted to enter Tibet, the city's gatekeeper stopped him and tried to convince him to go back to China. While the gatekeeper's attempts failed to persuade Lao Tzu to return to China, he did manage to persuade him to write down his thoughts on life. This is said to be how the Tao Te Ching came about. The following passages are excerpts from the Tao Te Ching and provide and insight into the working of Lao Tzu's mind and the Taoist religion:

Chapter 33
To understand others is to have knowledge;
To understand oneself is to be illumined.
To conquer others needs strength;
To conquer oneself is harder still.
To be content with what one has is to be rich.
He that works through violence may get his way;
But only what stays in its place can endure.
When one dies, one is not lost; there is no other longevity.

Chapter 44
Fame or one's own self, which matters to one most?
One's own self or things bought, which should count
    most?
In the getting or the losing, which is worse?
Hence he who grudges expense pays dearest in the end;

He who has hoarded will suffer the heaviest loss
Be content with what you have and are, and no one can
     despoil you;
Who stops in time nothing can harm.
He is forever safe and secure.

These segments from the Tao Te Ching show the importance of self-knowledge in Taoism, and of the need to realise the limited value of material possessions. These are philosophies are prominent in all the Eastern religions we have looked at so far as well as being ideas that often provide the subject matter for meditations today.

Taoism is similar to Zen Buddhism, as the best way to learn about it is to actually practise it, something that is done through regular meditation in a monastery or similar environment. To become a Taoist, followers must be intelligent, sensitive people who have the patience and attention span to be able to cope with long periods of meditation on often fairly abstract subjects.

Taoism can be considered from three different perspectives. At one level, Taoism is concerned with placing a definition on the true nature of existence. Existence in its purest form is said to be impossible for the human mind to comprehend, as our senses are considered too dull to understand something so complex. The ultimate reality is way beyond anything that humans can experience or understand. Tao is a vague concept that is said to be the source of all life

and creation. It is difficult to glean knowledge of
Taoism from studying or researching it from an abstract
perspective, and to learn more about it, it is really
necessary to practise Taoism. This is done by
meditation, which it is believed allows us to tap into
the unconscious mind. By accessing the unconscious
mind, it is said that we will behold the ultimate truth
of existence in a moment of enlightenment. Tao can be
considered as an infinite and everlasting entity, which
cannot be seen but never leaves us. It is believed to
have created everything and is said to be found within
each of us.

On another level, Taoism can be seen to express the
mystery there is surrounding nature and the universe.
Believers in Taoism see the Earth as being cyclical –
something which can be seen in the way the tides rises
and falls, the seasons change in a regular pattern, and
the sun rises and sets. There is a sense of balance in
nature and this is expressed by the Chinese as Yin and
Yang. Yang is the dominant, just force, while Yin is the
passive, merciful force. These two forces are in direct
competition but it is important that they stay balanced
as if one is allowed to exceed the other then the results
can be dangerous. These forces are also believed to be
present in each individual and if they exist in perfect
balance, then the person will be an ideal human being.
The main objective behind Taoism is that each
individual should live in harmony with Tao the creator
of all things, and with all creations, both animate and
inanimate. Taoism dictates that each follower should

follow the rules of Tao. This means that it is impossible for humans to seek to improve themselves or their surroundings in any way. Instead it is advocated that we should seek to live peaceful and contented lives, accepting what we are and what we have.

Finally, Taoism can be seen as a way of creating a perfect human. We have already mentioned that followers of Tao must attempt to live harmoniously with all living things, human and animal. There are two ways for someone to adhere to Taoism. The first is through an ascetic and reclusive lifestyle where the individual can renounce all earthly, material pleasures and go off on their own to contemplate and meditate on the nature of existence. If Tao exist throughout all life and creation then it is present in each of us so the only way to come to know Tao is to know oneself. In order to know oneself better it is necessary to meditate as that is the only way of tapping into our unconscious minds. The other form of Taoism is that available to the lay person who must earn a living and does not have the time for long periods of meditation. This person can follow Taoism through more practical methods such as going to church.

Followers of Taoism aspire to perfecting themselves by ridding themselves of all earthly desires for things such as sensual pleasure, material wealth, social status and power over others. This goal remains prevalent to some degree throughout many forms of meditation today. Taoists believe that perfection cannot be achieved by people who pursue such earthly things, and can only be achieved by someone who has rid themselves of these desires, stopped placing their own needs as the top priority, and who has lived a wholesome and useful life. The best way to achieve perfection is to go and live in a monastery and practice Taoism under the instruction of a master. This is an extremely difficult and demanding lifestyle and will only be mastered by those with much willpower and determination. The novice of Taoism will be instructed on how to practise yoga, on correct breathing techniques and on different ways to meditate.

Such novices can only be considered true followers of Taoism when they come to accept all aspects of nature and everything that happens to them as an integral part of existence as a whole. It is important that they are accommodating towards, and accepting of, life's changes whether these be good or bad. When they die they can take comfort in their belief that their soul will return to Tao, the source of their original creation, where they will be reborn as a new creation.

The essential components of a good life are believed to be simplicity, patience, the acceptance of our lot, and compassion towards others. There are no moral laws or commandments to prescribe to as there are in Christianity and Buddhism because followers of Tao see them as being unnecessary as goodness and virtue stems from inside all of us. Followers of Tao are expected to love both themselves and other people. They are said to refrain from trying to define ultimate values of good and evil or right and wrong as they recognise that all values are relative and cannot exist in isolation.

To conclude, Taoists are entirely accepting of all aspects of existence whether these are positive or negative. To become a follower of Tao, you must live a life of moderation, keeping control on your passions at all times. A life of balance is necessary if you wish to achieve perfection. All that you need to become a Taoist exists inside of you, so there is no need to attend church, or recite prayers or follow particular rituals. Taoists believe that if you truly look inside yourself – something that can be achieved through regular meditation sessions – you will find all that you need to know.

Hinduism

Another religion that practices meditation is Hinduism. Hinduism is the oldest of the major religions of the world with parts of the Hindu religion existing 2000 years before Christ. There are many religions that are considered to be a part of Hinduism – these include the Dharmas, Sikhs and Sanatanists. Indian people do not use the term Hindu to describe their own religion – this is a name made up by Europeans and comes from the Indus River that runs through Pakistan. Like Tao, the Hindu God is a nameless entity, who is believed to have created the universe. In order for humans to understand this God, he has been presented as having a human appearance and human characteristics in Hindu literature. Hindus therefore worship several Gods who can all be considered to represent different aspects of the single God who created the entire universe. A virtuous Hindu is one who does not commit theft or murder and one who practises honesty, charity and discipline and who shows kindness and understanding towards other humans.

Like Buddhism, Hinduism has close ties to nature and the Indians display a sense of reverence towards nature. These objects are said to be filled with spiritual power and the natural object that is considered to be the most sacred is the river Ganges which runs through the city of Varanasi. This is because it is believed that the Ganges originated when the goddess Ganga came through the heavens through the hair of the god Shiva in order to free the people. It is believed to be particularly sacred to bathe in the Ganges or, when you die, to have your body cremated on the banks of the river. This love of nature can also be seen in the Hindu's attitude towards cows. Cows are considered highly sacred and, if one were to wander onto the road, then motorists would just have to wait until it moved of its own free will. In the eyes of a Hindu, injuring a cow would be like injuring a god.

Like with Taoism, in Hinduism there is no single religious text to be followed in order to become a true Hindu. In fact, Hinduism is not comprised from a single set of beliefs. Within Hinduism there are several different sects who all worship different gods. This absence of one model of living means that like the other Eastern religions, Hindus are more tolerant of other people's religions. Although Hindus mainly worship within the home, many Hindus go to temples to pray and meditate. In temples, it is common to see Hindus praying in the lotus position in a trance-like state for up to hours at a time. In order to meditate in the Hindu way it is necessary to chant a mantra. You should also place your middle finger at the corner of one eye while the third finger is placed in the middle of the forehead.

There are many sources of literature for the Hindu religion. This includes the Veda epics, the Upanishads, the Puranas, the laws of Manu, the Bhagavad-Gita and the Ramanaya story. The Veda epics were first brought to India in 1500 BC by the Aryan people, who were originally from Persia, and these were also the inspiration for the creation of Transcendental Meditation, something that we shall look at in the next chapter. The Vedas were comprised of hymns and prayers composed in poetic language which described Hindu Gods and the battle they took part in. The Upanishads translates into English as 'The Wisdom of the Gurus'. These are a set of parables and dialogues which go some way towards explaining the Hindu's idea of the soul (atman) and how this relates to the universal soul (Brahman). Hindus believe that the individual human soul must be reincarnated a number of times before it can finally merge with the one universal soul Brahman. The soul is freed from this

endless reincarnation by god's deliverer, Moksa. Moksa
can free the soul through what is known as gnosis –
the secret knowledge that Hindus can find out about
through regularly practising meditation and yoga.

Hinduism began as a primitive form of nature
worship. Hindus believe that all things throughout the
universe are connected and all aspects of the world
whether animate or inanimate are symbols of God's
power to create. Hindus consider the material world to
be illusory and this is referred to as maya. Humans
cannot comprehend the ultimate reality of existence as
our powers of perception are considered to be too
limited. Hindus believe that humans are only capable
of seeing fragments of the complete reality of existence.

The ultimate goal of Hinduism is for the individual
soul of each human to be freed from continuous
reincarnation and to be united with the universal soul
Brahman. For this to happen, Hindus must liberate
themselves from the material world or maya, which is
the world that can be perceived by our senses. This
includes such negative emotions as anger, greed, lust
and the desire for power. For Hindus, there are two
ways to practise their religion. One way is suitable for
the lay person who, busy working for a living, has no
time to devote to meditation or yoga. This person is
referred to as a devotee. The other way is for so-called
yogis who, through regular meditation and yoga
practise, reach human perfection. As their as several
Gods within Hinduism – each representing a particular
aspect of the main God or source of all creation –

worshipping different Gods can mean different things. For example, Krishna at one point is said to have informed his friend, Ajuna, that salvation can be reached if one practises meditation, quells desire and gives up action. Therefore, if when Hindus meditate on Krishna, then the chance of their soul becoming united with Brahman, the universal soul, is far higher.

The key to good living is called Dharma, which is basically a collective name for the virtues that Hindus must display in life to reach salvation and unite their souls with Brahman. To complete this process of salvation, Hindus must follow four paths to the ultimate divine truth. The fourth path is entitled Moksha and is when this union of souls takes place. Hindus can complete this final stage by practising a number of different yogas. The performance of these yogas is called bhakti and these practises are designed to purify the body and soul, ridding them of all impure actions and thoughts. Bhakti is practised by Hindus referred to as bhaktas or devotees. To reach perfection, Hindus must strive to become yogis. Achieving this title means that they escape reincarnation and their souls are free to become united with Brahman. Meditation is used in the first of these yogas which is called raja yoga. Meditation is believed to be the method by which the physical senses are controlled to the point where the mind becomes oblivious to all outward sensations. Hindus meditate in order to receive a pure, intuitive form of knowledge that transcends all forms of sensory perception of the material world. The sense of personal identity must be diminished so that the person who is meditating can achieve a complete union with Brahman at a higher level of existence.

Christian Mysticism

Meditation is not only an integral part of these Eastern religions that we have looked at, but can also be found in religions closer to home such as Christianity. Consider the following excerpts:

> Neither shall they say, Lo here! Or Lo there!
> For, behold, the kingdom of God is within you.
> *Luke, chapter 17 verse, 21*

As with the Eastern religions, Christians also believe that in order to truly find God we have to look inside ourselves, and one way of doing this is through meditation. While Christianity is a highly structured religion combining regular attendance at church with the recital of prayers and hymns and other rituals, these are useless if they are simply followed without true feeling or sincerity. It is understandable why there is evidence of meditation in Christianity throughout the ages.

The following passage is taken from *The Cloud of Unknowing*, a text from the 14th century:

> Just as the meditations of those who seek to live

the contemplative life come without warning, so, too, do their prayers. I am thinking of their private prayers, of course, not those laid down by the Holy Church. For true contemplatives could not value such prayers more, and so they use them, in the form and according to the rules laid down by the holy fathers before us, But their own personal prayers rise spontaneously to God, without bidding of premeditation, beforehand or during their prayer.

From The Cloud of Unknowing, *Chapter 37*

Meditation is particularly evident in the branch of Christianity known as mysticism. This part of Christianity has been around for centuries, and mystics believe that meditation is a more effective way of getting to know God than through more regimented ways of practising religion such as reciting prayers and taking part in debates. The word 'mysticism' comes from the Greek word 'mustikos' meaning 'initiated person.' The best way to describe a mystic is a person who transcends everyday reality and becomes familiar with the mysteries of existence, achieving a union with God through meditation.

A mystical experience is when an individual feels a union with God in a spontaneous moment of epiphany without having planned it or having striven to achieve it. This is an instinctive, intuitive feeling rather then a rational experience. It can happen during a time of heightened emotion or trauma but it is said to happen more often during solitary meditation. At the height of this experience, the person feels as though they have become one with God and does feel any distinction between their individual personality and God.

Mystics therefore do not require to attend church or adhere to more formalised religious rituals as they have all that they need to know God within themselves. As it requires much time to devote to long sessions of meditation, most people do not have the time to become mystics and choose to practise more structured forms of worship. Neither do they have the dedication required to renounce all worldly pleasures and exercise such strict discipline over the body and mind.

One of the most famous mystics was St Francis of Assisi who came to religion when believed that he witnessed a vision of the crucified Christ. This led him to forsake worldly goods, devote his life to charitable deeds, and travel about preaching the word of God. Like Buddha, he felt an enormous affiliation with all creatures and fostered the pantheistic belief that God was present throughout all living things. This belief that all living things should be respected as a gift of creation is still held by many people who practise meditation today.

CHAPTER 5
Transcendental Meditation

Transcendental Meditation is one of the most popular forms of alternative therapy that there is. I have chosen to dedicate an entire chapter to the discussion of Transcendental Meditation because it is perhaps the most appropriate form of meditation to meet the needs of people who have a Western way of life. Furthermore, this is by far the most popular form of meditation practised in the West, not to mention the most obviously scientific.

Transcendental Meditation was founded in 1958 by Maharishi Mahesh Yogi. Maharishi means 'sage, or 'wise one'. The idea for Transcendental Meditation comes from the Vedas or songs of wisdom – the ancient Hindu scriptures that we discussed in the last chapter. The Maharishi learned Transcendental Meditation from Swami Brahmananda Saraswati, a Hindu monk, who before his death in 1953, persuaded the Maharishi to teach this discipline to others.

Transcendental Meditation has many features that distinguish it from other forms of meditation. Other schools of meditation, such as Buddhist meditation can often be seen to encourage the individual who is practising it to live an often reclusive life devoting to the learning of yoga and meditation techniques whilst renouncing a life guided by worldly desires and goals. With TM, however, there is quite a different approach. Proponents of TM do not believe that it will enhance their lives by distancing themselves from the worldly reality of life in the way that some Buddhists do when they meditate on impermanence, for example.

While TM is seen as a way of promoting the spiritual side of each individual, it is also believed to deal with the reality of life in a very practical way. For example, the Maharishi has stated that the goals of meditation amongst other things are to improve the efficacy of the government, reach the highest ideals of education, solve the social problems that humans encounter such as drug abuse and poverty and improve the economic conditions of the world. The Maharishi has demonstrated a hands-on approach to solving these solutions and has regular interviews with the press and even offered his solution to the Persian Gulf Crisis in 1990. He has also invited all governments to use his teachings and theories to improve the operation of the countries that they govern and has also has held several assemblies on world peace in many countries throughout the world. He has also developed a course designed for leaders of political parties, which is based on his theories of Natural Law, and which he claims will teach them the ideal method of administration that will create a perfect government. TM is suitable for a constantly changing modern day society in a way that other schools of meditation are not. For example, the Maharishi has developed courses that aim to improve efficiency and boost profitability in corporate companies.

Maharishi Mahesh Yogi has complete faith in his theories of meditation and encourages scientific scrutiny. His own scientific background (he has a degree in physics) has allowed him to present his theories in a very scientific way. In Transcendental Meditation literature, the findings of experiments where physiological changes in those who meditate are presented - such as changes in the frequency of brain waves, changes in metabolism, galvanic skin response, and decreased heart rate. Supporting his technique with scientific evidence has probably contributed to the widespread success of the Maharashi's theories. The Mahirishi believes in the power of natural law, which he compares to the laws of physics. This basically states that there is a force of energy that runs through all of nature and through this arises the set of laws that govern nature. This means that there is an infinite amount of energy, creativity and intelligence running through all of us and through TM he claims that we can tap into this for our own use. This is another reason why TM is particularly recommended to students and schoolchildren – not only does it help them to relax during stressful periods such as exam time, but it also stimulates thought and creativity.

While TM does not require that people convert to a

particular religion, the Maharishi is obviously
influenced by Hindu texts. On completion of his
degree, the Maharishi spent 13 years as a Hindu monk
under the instruction of Swami Brahmananda
Saraswati. As well as basing TM on the Vedas, he also
completed a commentary on the Bhagavad-Gita. He
spent a further two years living as a hermit before
embarking on a teaching mission that would see
Transcendental Meditation taking off all round the
world. Instead of confining his teaching to India, he
had the visionary idea of spreading it to more
technologically advanced countries such as the USA
and he flew into San Francisco in 1959 – a trip that
would be the beginning of a huge phenomenon
throughout the USA. He began to teach TM around the
world in 1959 and, in 1960, he began a three-year
plan that aimed to spiritually regenerate the world. The
spread of TM throughout the world was also enhanced
when, in 1960, the Maharishi began to train teachers
who could then go on to teach meditation in his place.
In fact, if you look up TM on the Internet, you will
find official TM websites for several different countries.
He took advantage of modern methods of
communication and this combined with his logical,
scientific approach to explicating his theories has led to
the huge success of Transcendental Meditation
throughout the world.

This form of meditation became increasingly
popular in the West throughout the '60s when the
hippie movement emerged and people became more

and more concerned with spiritual growth. TM is not only popular in the West but the Maharishi's theories have enjoyed success in many other countries throughout the world and the writings of the Maharishi have been translated into many different languages. Transcendental Meditation had many proponents including famous figures such as the Beatles. An estimated 4 million people in the world – almost 200,000 people in the UK – now practice Transcendental Meditation. In fact, it is said that a group of doctors in the UK actually sent a petition to the government to request that TM become more readily available on the National Health Service.

The first official international academy for Transcendental Meditation was set up in 1966, and there now exists many schools where people can go to more about TM, including 80 schools in the UK where lectures and courses are held throughout the year. The Maharishi also established universities in 1993 where people can go to learn about the theories that lie behind his technique of TM. The number of people who have taken up Transcendental Meditation is probably far larger if it were possible to count all of the people who are self-taught through books and videos but have not actually attended a course at one of these schools. The Maharishi himself estimates that one-percent of the population practise meditation. On top of this, it is estimated that a further 100,000 people in the world have learned the Maharishi's Yogic Flying. This technique is said to be even more effective than

TM and is a meditation method that revives the art of yoga – a practice that we will discuss in chapter 14.

Transcendental Meditation has continued to be a success in the West since its introduction in the '60s because it is highly scientific and it very simple to practice. All proponents of TM have to do is meditate twice a day for 20-minute spells – once in the morning and again in the evening. Many people who practise meditation claim that even though they may have a busy life, it is worth putting these 20-minute slots aside as the rest of the day becomes so much more productive. It is claimed that meditation makes people more effective and energised, and so less time is needed to spend on tasks that would normally take much time and mental effort. Although the Maharishi is a Hindu, his followers can be of any religion or no religion at all. The main purpose of Transcendental Meditation is to improve the quality of life of the person who practices it, regardless of their religious beliefs. TM is also considered to be a holistic practice. For example, if you go to the doctor with a sore head, then he or she will more than likely give you medicine to treat that particular ailment. This will probably be in the form of a painkiller that will only mask the pain instead of pinpointing the source in order to remove it altogether. TM, however, is said to treat the entire body and mind, as the two are seen as being interconnected, and if one is unhealthy then this is believed to have a knock-on effect on the other. This holistic approach can also be seen in the Maharishi's view of society, which is that problems in society are caused by a sense of malaise throughout society and that an individual's feelings of stress can have an adverse affect on society as a whole.

Transcendental meditation is also said to be extremely easy to learn and pleasurable to practise. It is entirely natural and, like most forms of meditation, it requires no props of any kind. This form of meditation is also said to be suitable for anyone of ten years or over, and it is taught and practised in many seemingly unlikely places. TM is said to be particularly helpful to different groups of society. For example, more courses are being run in places like corporate firms, prisons and even schools. It is also said to be beneficial for prisoners who are being rehabilitated and it is believed that it can help to prevent re-offending. It is also claimed that TM can be beneficial for couples who wish to work on their relationship, for convalescents who are recovering from serious illnesses and for even for employees of companies whose directors wish them to become more efficient. It is also recommended for people who have chronic addiction to substances of any kind, such as alcoholics and drug addicts, as it has been shown that TM not only helps people stop abusing substances, but also helps them to continue to stay off them on a long-term basis. Many athletes have also taken up meditation in order to improve their performance. This is because TM is thought to improve reaction times, mind-body co-ordination, prevent nerves and so improve performance in general. It is not necessary to belong to a particular group. Even if you have no special needs, proponents of TM believe it can help you. People who practise TM on a regular basis are said to be more spontaneous, more accepting of themselves, more able to develop warm relationships with others, more flexible in their approach to life and have higher self-regard than people who do not practise TM.

It is emphasised that with TM there is no need to place any strain on the body and it is not physically demanding in anyway. There is also no need to manipulate the body into positions that can initially seem difficult or uncomfortable – positions that are often recommended for other forms of meditation. TM does not involve having to concentrate or direct the mind in any way. It is also said to be possible to practise meditation anywhere – something that is not always recommended to beginners in other forms of meditation.

While the Maharishi is a highly prominent and respected figure, he makes no claim to possessing supernatural power and his down-to-earth character and the emphasis he places on a scientific approach sets him apart from other Eastern gurus. This had led to emphasis being placed on the technique employed in Transcendental Meditation, drawing attention away from the figurehead of this discipline. The technique itself is highly simple – all it involves is the mental repetition of a Sanskrit word referred to as a mantra. We will discuss the mantra in greater depth in chapter 9.

The Oxford English Dictionary provides the following definition for transcend:

Transcend: *v.tr.* **1** beyond the range or grasp of (human experience; reason, belief, etc.) **2.** Excel; surpass.

To attempt to go beyond the realms of everyday existence is exactly what this method of meditation involves. This is achieved by way of a technique that allows the mind to become calm and relaxed whilst remaining alert and aware. The goal of TM is to reach what is referred to as pure consciousness. Reaching this state is said to occur when we are allowed to access the unconscious and the source of all our conscious thoughts. Transcendental Meditation does not only relax the mind, but as a result of the deepened state of relaxation achieved when the practitioner reaches pure awareness, the body is seen to become relaxed as well. Thus, the goals of TM are not unlike the goals of other forms of meditation that we have looked at – to relax the body whilst heightening the consciousness.

The technique involved in TM is to repeat a mantra that is usually a Sanskrit word that has been chosen for us by our instructor. People who practise Transcendental Meditation are able to go beyond the stresses and strains of everyday life allowing them to increase their self-knowledge and self-awareness. By continuous repetition of a word or mantra, we will achieve conscious awareness of that thought. This feeling of conscious awareness will intensify and we will then achieve what this state of pure consciousness – a state which he claims will also us to access much energy and intelligence. It is basically thinking about something but being oblivious to external factors and reaching a state of complete awareness. This is something that practitioners of TM believe is a natural state of mind, but due to being caught up in the stress of our daily lives, we have lost the ability to reach this state of mind – TM is said to put us back in touch with this.

To achieve this pure consciousness, we would be required to focus our attention on the repetition of the word or mantra, just as we will focus our attention on the sound of our own breathing or on a mental image in other forms of meditation. The mantra should not be repeated aloud but silently in the mind. The eyes should be kept shut at all times. Just as with other meditations, in TM it is important that we do not strive to hard to keep attention focussed on the object of the meditation – the repetition of the word or mantra. When you try this, your mind will inevitably wander, but with practise this should happen less and you will become quicker at redirecting the attention to the repetition of the mantra. As with other meditations, TM will become more productive with practise. Once achieved, the state of pure awareness will be easier to recreate during future meditations.

We have already mentioned that this technique is suitable for people of all religions as there is no stress placed on devotional meaning but rather on repetition of the mantra to achieve pure consciousness. At times, your attention will lose sight of the mantra and become distracted by thoughts and images that will emerge in your consciousness. According to the Maharishi, this shows that accumulated stress is being gradually released from your mind.

If you decide to take up Transcendental Meditation, it is necessary that you meditate for two 20-minute periods – one in the morning and one at night. It is also important that you wait for a couple of hours after having a meal before you begin to meditate. Other than this, you are not required to make any changes to your lifestyle, a feature of TM that makes it particularly suitable for Westerners with hectic lifestyles. The Maharishi believes that regular meditation will cause changes in life-style to come about anyway. This is due to the belief that the feeling of deep relaxation and pure consciousness during meditation will inevitably be carried into normal daily life and will have a positive effect on this. The Maharishi believes that when one meditates for several years, eventually the state that is achieved during meditation will be present at all times throughout the day.

Despite being a simple discipline, Transcendental Meditation is widely believed to carry immense benefits for the body and mind. The benefits of practising Transcendental Meditation include reduced levels of stress, improved personal relationships, improved health, greater personal effectiveness, and increased self-knowledge. Proponents of TM do not claim that it will remove sources of stress in your life, but it will make them far easier to deal with. Stress is not caused by a difficult or demanding situation, but it is in fact caused by the way we react to one. It is also believed to increase the IQ, increased individual creativity, improve the ability to comprehend and focus, improve perception and memory and enhance orderliness of thought processes. These psychological and physical benefits that proponents of TM claim it brings about are summarised below:

Psychological benefits
- Improved cognitive powers
- Greater clarity of thought
- More effective problem solving
- More effective decision making
- Quicker reactions
- Improved confidence
- A greater sense of well-being
- Enhanced intelligence
- Enhanced creativity
- Improved memory
- Improved ability to learn
- Heightened alertness
- Greater comprehension
- The ability to concentrate
- Alleviation of anxiety
- Alleviation of depression

Physical benefits

- A greater sense of relaxation
- Alleviation of stress
- Greater levels of energy
- Greater levels of stamina
- Less chance of developing heart disease
- Reduced cholesterol levels
- Reduced levels of hypertension
- Fewer problems with weight gain
- Reduced chronic fatigue
- Psychosomatic problems alleviated
- Less chance of contracting a disease or illness
- Less dependence on substances such as alcohol, cigarettes, or drugs
- A strengthened immune system
- Less difficulty in falling asleep
- A deeper, more productive sleep
- Less headaches

In fact, many studies have been done to support the theory that Transcendental Meditation is beneficial – the publicity generated by these studies is another factor that has boosted the popularity of TM. Since the first scientific research done on TM was carried out in 1970, over 500 studies have been carried out which support the claims that TM is beneficial to the mind, body, behaviour and society in general. These studies have taken various different factors into account, and have looked at the benefits of TM from physiological, behavioural and sociological perspectives. Many of these studies have used rigorous methods of research. Findings of experiments have also been backed up with the findings of other experiments. These studies have been carried out in over 200 universities in 33 different countries, including Harvard Medical School, the University of Edinburgh, the University of New South Wales and the Institute de la Rochfoucauld in France.

When people practise TM, it has been proven that alpha and theta brain waves emerge in the central and rear cortex and then continue to spread to the frontal lobes. This effect has rarely been seen as a result of any other relaxation technique or drug and indicates that the person is both relaxed and alert, thus highlighting a major difference between brain activity during meditation and brain activity during sleep. The left and right hemispheres of the brain are also shown to work in a more synchronised manner that is also rarely seen in the human brain. This mental activity goes some way towards supporting the theory that practitioners of TM have greater cognitive powers and more clarity of thought.

Transcendental Meditation is different from other forms of meditation as it requires no effort and is all down to technique. When practising TM, breathing becomes slower and more shallow automatically as a result of the state of relaxation that the practitioner reaches. It has also been shown that blood pressure and even cholesterol levels have diminished in subjects who have taken up TM on a regular basis. Studies also show that heart rate can slow down up to 15%, thus taking the strain off of the entire cardiovascular system. It has also been shown that people who practise TM on a regular basis have lower levels of blood lactate and cortisol – chemicals that are produced in the body when under stress. They have also been shown to have higher levels of positive chemicals such as plasma prolactin and phenylanolin, thus supporting the theory that TM can boost the general functioning of the body.

There is also medical evidence to suggest that various muscle groups in the body automatically become relaxed as a result of TM, further supporting the theory that TM is effective in reducing stress. There is also evidence to suggest that practising TM boosts the immune system and lessens the chance of contracting illnesses and life-threatening diseases such as cancer. There have also been studies that support the claim that practising TM can reduce the need for by-pass operations and medical treatment in general. Practitioners of TM have pointed out that if the need for medical treatment of illness was diminished then millions of pounds that are spent treating illness could be ploughed into the prevention of illness. There is also much evidence to show that TM is an invaluable aid when overcoming addiction. Furthermore, it has been claimed that TM can slow down ageing. This is due to the fact that stress can cause premature ageing in humans, so when the stress is relieved then it can no longer accelerate the ageing process.

There have also been several scientific studies carried out that compared the benefits of TM with the benefits of other forms of relaxation. These showed evidence to suggest that TM was more successful than other forms of meditation when it came to eliminating stress. Studies have also been done to indicate that TM was of more benefit when overcoming addictions, improving mental and physical health and when increasing individual potential. The claim that creativity increases as a result of practising TM on a regular basis has also been supported by scientific study. Such studies involved carious tests of verbal, pictorial fluency. Those who practise TM are also said to have outperformed those who do not practise it in memory tests

This scientific research does not just support the theory that TM has a beneficial effect on a person's physical and mental well being. There have also been studies done which show that TM can also have a positive effect on the environment and can even promote world peace. This theory was proposed in 1975 and was labelled the Maharishi Effect. For example, in areas where one percent of the population practise TM, it has been shown that there are lower levels of crime and fewer traffic accidents. The explanation for this phenomenon is that when individuals become less stressed and more creative they have a far more useful contribution to make to society. The Maharishi believes there is a collective consciousness, and that each individual can therefore exert an influence on that consciousness in a positive or a negative manner. Just as we can all benefit from tapping into the creative life force that flows throughout nature, we can also be adversely affected by the tension that stressed individuals give off. The larger the number of stressed individuals, the more likely it is that that stress will spread. Many proponents of TM therefore believe that the problems of society, such as crime, violence, poverty and drug abuse, are caused by a feeling of stress in the collective consciousness rather than just being down to the actions of a number of individuals.

The holistic nature of Transcendental Meditation is perhaps why it has become so popular in the workplace, with many company directors providing courses in TM for their employees in order to boost a flagging workforce. In fact, one study was carried out in a large company in America that showed that employee performance improved dramatically once employees took up meditation. There was also said to be less complaints of poor health amongst employees, improved job satisfaction for employees and increased co-operation between employees.

Proponents of TM stress that it is not a case of taking up a different lifestyle when taking up meditation on a regular basis but a way of enhancing the lifestyle you already possess. There is no need to shave your head, to wear saffron robes, to give up hobbies you enjoy or only associate with other people who meditate. TM is no religion or cult. With TM, there is no need to become reclusive in order to reap the benefits – something which more religion-based forms of meditation can involve. Neither is it seen as a way of escaping reality and the problems that go with it, as people who practice TM are said to be better at dealing with what life throws at them. In fact, teachers of meditation stress that there is no need to change your lifestyle in any way, other than finding time to meditate for two 20-minute sessions each day.

Proponents of TM also believe that it allows them to make greater use of their cognitive powers. It is estimated that on average most of us only use around five to ten percent of our brains. This is because TM is said to allow us to tap into our unconscious, the place where all our conscious thoughts come from. It does this as it quietens the mind, taming the distracting flow of thoughts that prevent us from delving deep enough to reach our unconscious. It is also believed that TM can make us more efficient people in our day-to-day lives. This is based on the fact that our behaviour is controlled by our thoughts. Therefore, if TM can clarify the mind and strengthen the power of our mental processes, then this will automatically have positive effects on our behaviour.

We have seen that Transcendental Meditation does not adhere to any religion or make use of devotional practises and it entirely based on technique. In fact, people of all kinds of religion practise TM without having to compromise any beliefs that they possess. It is even said to be beneficial for those people with religious beliefs as it increases awareness and so may help religious people enhance their spirituality and even allow them to feel a greater connection with their idea of God. In fact, if you go into any bookshop, you are likely to find many books that combine the benefits of TM with the religion of Christianity. We have also seen that TM is not a complicated philosophical theory but a very simple technique that is backed up with straightforward scientific evidence.

For details of these studies and for more information on Transcendental Meditation in general, you can visit the UK website at: www.transcendental-meditation.org.uk.

Chapter 6
Starting Off: Preparing to Meditate

In general, meditation is a simple process and, despite what many people believe, there is little to learn. As we discussed earlier, it is not necessary to be initiated by a teacher, nor is it necessary to adopt uncomfortable poses. The most important factor in becoming adept at meditation is practise. It is therefore advisable to incorporate meditation into your daily routine. Meditating for a short spell on a daily basis is far more effective then meditating for an hour once a week. Once you have begun meditating, you will notice that even a short break from it will mean that it may be more difficult when you go back to it.

You will remember that we previously defined meditation as a combination of a deep state of relaxation and a heightened consciousness or awareness. There is no need to go into a trance - a state many people associate with meditation. You will remain fully in control of your actions and will able to end the meditation at any time you wish. You will also remember the meditation afterwards.

It is important to remember that meditation is a

personal experience and once you have mastered the basics you can tailor them to suit your individual needs. If a particular method benefits you then keep at it. On the other hand, if it starts to make you feel uncomfortable then you can stop at any time. You should not waste time working towards goals or concentrating on the future as this distracts you from the present, which is what we should be concerning ourselves with.

It is also important to realise that meditation does not start when you actively sit down to meditate and then finish when you get back up. Once you have started meditating, it is more helpful to consider it as a lifestyle. The actual process of meditation is the time to focus on your thoughts and the rest of your life is an opportunity to use your new found awareness and use this to pinpoint changes you wish to make to your life.

Preparing to Meditate

There are seven basic factors, which should be taken into consideration as you prepare to meditate:

- Physical and mental comfort
- Posture/Position
- Breathing
- Stimuli
- Awareness
- Surroundings
- Duration

Physical and Mental Comfort

When meditating, it is important that you be comfortable as physical and/or mental discomfort render successful meditation impossible. It is a good idea to wear loose, non-restrictive clothing and to adopt a comfortable position. Ties, belts or any other restrictive clothing should be loosened or removed. We have already dismissed the notion that it is necessary to adopt a difficult or uncomfortable position, so just choose whichever one suits you best. Try not to get too comfortable, however as you may find that you fall asleep. Also make sure that you have enough clothes on to avoid feeling cold, but be careful that you do not wear too many layers as if you are too warm, it can make you feel sleepy and less alert.

Some people find that taking a bath is a useful precursor to meditation as warm water helps the muscles relax and rids us of some of the stress that accumulates throughout the day whilst eliminating aches and pains that can cause discomfort and hinder meditation. It is also a good idea to blow the nose and visit the toilet before the meditation as stopping the meditation to empty the bladder means that you have to start all over again.

Unless you are using some kind of external stimulus then it is probably best to keep the eyes shut during meditation. This lessens the risk of distraction. If you feel uncomfortable during the meditation, then do not be scared to alleviate whatever is causing the discomfort. If you have an itch then scratch it, if you need to visit the toilet then so do. It may mean that you have to begin the meditation all over again, but this is better than carrying on in discomfort.

Posture/Position

Assuming a particular posture is considered important in most schools of meditation. As I have already mentioned, correct breathing is the key to successful meditation so it is important not to slouch as this can hinder breathing. Whatever position you choose to mediate in, it is important to keep a straight back and this is considered important in all traditions of meditation. It is also important to keep the head upright and facing straight ahead. To correct a bad posture, imagine that you are balancing books on your head. This is a task that requires you to remain with your shoulders back and your spine straight. If you have a particularly bad posture, then this may feel very uncomfortable to begin with. The spine will be used to curling round and it may be quite painful to suddenly straighten it out. However, this will definitely be worth it in the end. A correct posture is not just vital for a successful meditation but has many other benefits for health in general. It allows you to breathe more effectively and can help you to avoid back problems in later life. It also conveys a more positive and confident attitude to other people, so it is worth trying to achieve.

When you meditate with a straight spine, the

weight of the body becomes evenly distributed and the body is given a sense of balance by the pull of gravity. This means that the muscles are used less. It has been suggested that this stable sense of balance has a positive affect on the state of mind although this has never been proven. Maintaining a straight back during meditation is often referred to as poised posture. Poised posture helps to promote the state of mind necessary for meditation – mentally alert but relaxed at the same time.

A sitting position is probably the most suitable position for a beginner. This is because it is easy to achieve and there is less danger of you falling asleep than there would be if you were to lie down. It is not necessary to adopt one of the more traditional Eastern postures but if you plan to take up meditation on a long-term basis, it is worth trying them out as they do ensure an excellent basis for meditation. If you are supple enough, the traditional lotus or cross-legged positions are effective in providing a still and stable base on which to meditate. This allows the individual to remain comfortable while preventing the risk of falling over or losing balance. It also ensures that you remain alert and eliminates the risk of falling asleep. As the back remains straight, breathing is not hindered and the blood can circulate freely around the body.

If adopting either of these positions, remember to rest your knees on the floor, as this is important for stability. Furthermore, feel free to use cushions if this increases your comfort at all. If these positions are uncomfortable for you, do not worry. It is just as effective to sit on a chair or against a wall. As long as you are comfortable, the spine stays straight and you remain stationary that is enough. When you first start out, it is a good idea to practise sitting in different positions to find the correct one for you.

Here are some common positions that can be adopted when meditating:

- SITTING ON A CHAIR OR 'EGYPTIAN POSTURE'
  Perhaps one of the simplest positions in which to meditate is sitting in a straight-backed chair. Sit as far back on the chair as you can and rock back and forth in order to find the position where your weight presses most firmly onto the seat. If you are unsure of where this is, you can place your fingers underneath your buttocks to get a better idea. You should then remove your finger from underneath your buttocks and place them either one on each thigh or rest them lightly in your lap. This should stop you from fidgeting. Sit with the back spine straight against the back of the chair although try not to make your posture too rigid or you will not be able to fully relax. Your shoulders should be back and your head facing straight ahead. Imagine a string attached to the top of your head pulling your spine straighter and keeping your head level.

- CROSS-LEGGED
  Sit with your legs crossed and your knees as close

to the ground as is comfortable. Again, keep your back straight and your head facing straight ahead and cup your hands in your lap. This is a good position to adopt in preparation for the lotus position. You will find that the more you practice this, the closer your knees will be to the ground. Feel free to use a mat or cushion if it makes this position more comfortable.

- KNEELING WITH FEET TUCKED UNDER BUTTOCKS OR THE SEIZA POSITION

  Kneel down sitting on the inside of your heels. As with the previous position, it is vital to keep the spine straight and face straight ahead. As always, you can use a mat for comfort or even place a cushion between the buttocks and the heels. You can also use a specially designed bench. The hands can be cupped in the lap as before or one placed on each knee.

- HALF LOTUS

  This is a very effective position to meditate in as it is said to:
  - Relax and stabilise the nervous system,
  - Ease the tensions and stiffness in the joints and muscles, particularly the thighs, knees and ankles,
  - Provide a comfortable and stable position that promotes mental awareness from which to meditate.

Sit down with your legs stretched out in front of you. Bend your left knee and holding your left ankle, pull the left foot in so that the sole of the foot is resting against the top of your right inner thigh. The heel should be resting against the perineum. Your left knee should be firm against the floor with the right leg stretched out in front of the body. Now bend your right knee so that your right foot can then be pulled in towards the body. The right foot should be positioned so that it rests on the opposite thigh with the sole facing upwards. Again, maintain a straight spine and face straight ahead. Your knees should be as close to the floor as comfortably possible, If your legs become stiff when you first begin to attempt this, you can come out of the position and give them a rub. For some variation, you can also try the position with the right leg pulled in first and the left leg on top. It is important to vary the position of your legs as it means that both legs will become equally supple and you will then be ready to move on and try the full lotus position.

- LOTUS
  The benefits of the lotus position are:
  - This is the ideal sitting position for meditations of a longer duration. It gives a perfect sense of balance, and allows you to remain mentally alert – an essential precursor to meditation

- Regular use of this position leads to greater flexibility in joints and muscles. This in itself can aid relaxation and promote meditation.

This is a very difficult position to achieve and is more suitable for those who have been meditating for some time or for those who are already proficient in yoga. This is very similar to the half lotus but harder to achieve, so if you cannot do the half lotus effectively then you will not be able to do this.

The only difference between the lotus and the half lotus is that in the lotus, the right foot should be positioned on the left thigh with the sole facing upwards and the left foot should be positioned in the same way on the right thigh. The knees should both be touching the mat. The hands can either be placed on the knees with palms facing upwards, or can rest in the lap. As with the other positions, the back should remain straight and the head facing forwards. If you become stiff at all, then straighten out your legs and rub them down until the stiffness lessens.

This is perhaps the most famous position for meditating in and is the one most commonly used in traditional Eastern meditation. It is less commonly used in the West but if you have the time to practise it, it is worth learning as it gives a perfect sense of balance and stability to promote a successful meditation. It also increases the flexibility of joints and tones the leg muscles. Remember to vary the way that you cross you legs, so that each leg becomes more toned and flexible.

- BURMESE POSTURE
  This is one of the easier positions and it is therefore suitable for a beginner. In this position you do not cross the legs but instead the knees should be bent and resting close to the floor. The feet should be pulled back so that they are in front of the pelvis and one foot should remain in front of the other. The hands should be placed one on top of each thigh or cupped on top of the heels. It is necessary to push the buttocks out a little to allow you to sit with a straight spine. It is also a good idea to use a cushion or a mat to sit on to prevent you from becoming uncomfortable.

The following positions are also possible although these are said to be more suitable for someone who has been meditating for some time and has greater powers of concentration:

- WALKING MEDITATION
  This is a good way of meditating if you are on the move and do not have time for a sitting meditation. A walking meditation is made up of slow, small steps. The spine should remain straight as in a sitting meditation and the eyes should be open and facing straight ahead. To give you something to focus your awareness on, you can also count each

step while meditating. Whenever your attention wanders, simply direct it back to concentrating on the process of walking. Count from one to ten and then start again from the beginning. After about ten metres, you can change position. This is a good meditation to practise in your back garden or somewhere similar, as it is necessary to choose somewhere you will not be disturbed.

- STANDING MEDITATION

  The standing meditation is used by the Taoists can is referred to as embracing the pillar. You should stand with a straight back and you head facing directly ahead and your chin tucked in. Feet should be kept fairly close together and hands can either be places at your sides or rest gently on the abdomen. This is an excellent meditation for keeping a straight posture and remaining alert. Try to feel the gravity travel through your entire body and pull you down into the ground.

- EATING MEDITATION

  You can do this in a sitting or a standing position. For this meditation, it is best to use organic, whole-foods that have not been chemically treated in any way. You can meditate on a feeling of gratitude that you have food to eat, or you can choose to focus on the eating process – the tasting, chewing and then swallowing of the food. As digestion can distract us from the meditative process, this meditation is not recommended for beginners and is more suitable for someone who has been meditating for some time.

Once you have found a position to suit you, it is time to begin. If you are sitting, then concentrate on feeling balanced. Find a point of your body and imagine that it is the centre of your balance. Focus on this body part.

Breathing

We have already considered the role that breathing has in successful meditation, but this cannot be stressed enough. Oxygen is one of the greatest necessities in life, so to be deprived of oxygen is inevitably going to be bad for the health. If the body or mind is in a state of exertion, for example during a run, or a panic attack, we involuntary react by increasing our breathing rate. Thus it is also possible to voluntarily increase the amount of oxygen that we imbibe, thereby allowing the body to function more effectively and with reduced heart rate and blood pressure. Breathing is a psychological and physiological aid – breathing deeply automatically aids relaxation. This can be used in any situation in life where you are over anxious about something and would like to relax.

While meditating, it is best to breathe through the nostrils rather than the mouth. Breathe slowly and deeply, filling the lungs to their fullest capacity. As you inhale, your abdomen should distend slightly and then flatten again when you exhale. This is caused by the movement of your diaphragm as you breathe.

Stimuli

It can also be useful to have an object on which to concentrate on. Buddhists refer to this use of an object to keep the attention focussed on as achieving mindfulness, and consider it an essential way of keeping the mind alert and focussed. When selecting a suitable object, you should make sure that this object will remain in the vicinity for the duration of your meditation or it may prove distracting. This stimulus can be one of many things: an object in the room; a sound in the background; a feeling of contentment or even the sound of your own breathing. Any concrete or abstract object that you can focus attention on for 15 to 30 minutes while meditating can be used successfully. You will find that during your meditation, the mind will inevitably wander, but it is important that it has some sort of stimulus to come back to and focus the attention on.

Awareness

The mind should be alert and focused on the meditative experience. This is why factors such as comfort and surroundings are so important as distractions can stop alertness from being fully achieved. You should also try to forget about daily activities for the time being as it will be hard to fully concentrate on meditation if you are subconsciously listening out for the oven timer to sound or the telephone to ring.

During meditation, conscious concentration should become effortless. The stimulus which you focus should remain in the background ready to return to the foreground of the consciousness whenever your attention wanders too far and you wish to become focussed again. When you reach a complete state of awareness, the mind will be completely unaware of any external object having transcended all earthly things and will not be concentrating on anything. Awareness of the inner consciousness will be complete.

It is impossible to eliminate all distractions but as long as your awareness of them remains passive, it will not hinder meditation. You will find that the mind will repeatedly wander from the stimulus and this is perfectly acceptable. Whenever you become aware of this simply turn your attention back to the stimulus and this will refocus your mind. If you try to hard, this will cause stress and hinder the meditation process, When other thoughts flow into your mind simply acknowledge them before returning your focus to your chosen stimulus. The deeper into the meditation you go, the less likely you will be to be distracted by random thoughts.

Periods of sensory deprivation can cause hallucinations but these are highly unlikely to occur during a short, 20-minute meditation. If this does happen, do not be alarmed. Just acknowledge the experience and continue in your meditation. If you experience anything that makes you feel uncomfortable, then it is best to end the meditation. Simply allow yourself to gradually become aware of your external surroundings and the meditation will end.

It is imperative that you are not under the influence of any drugs, prescription or otherwise, when meditating. At best, drugs alter perceptions and affect the alertness of the mind, thus hindering meditation. At worse, the mind-altering effects of drugs combined with meditation could cause powerful hallucinations that could prove distressing. Meditation provides a safe and natural alternative to drugs in providing a method of relaxation. It costs less money and is not addictive and, as I have mentioned previously, it is also an effective way of combating an addiction.

Awareness during meditation should remain effortless but deliberate. If it requires effort to achieve then the meditation will not be successful. This may sound like a paradox, but it is something that comes with practice and it possible to achieve. You should allow the mind to remain conscious and alert but you should not strive for this to happen – it should come about naturally. Try not to be daunted if you find this hard to begin with. Consider an experienced driver. She does not need to go though every thought process when driving. When speeding up, she knows when to change gear automatically, unlike the beginner who requires to consciously observe what speed she is travelling at before deciding which gear is suitable. It is the same when we are meditating. The more adept you become, the less difficult it is to be relaxed without becoming sleepy, and to remain alert, but no so alert that thoughts start racing through your head.

If practised regularly, meditation will become effortless and you will experience increasingly prolonged periods of awareness, which are unhampered by distracting thoughts. The secret is not to try too hard – it is as simple as that. Once you have mastered this and managed to maintain the correct degree of awareness, meditation becomes a more productive and rewarding experience. Simply practise for 15 to 30 minutes, once or twice a day and you will soon begin to reap the benefits.

Surroundings

When choosing a place to meditate, it is usually best to choose a quiet tranquil environment that you can use on a regular basis. Successful meditation can only come about if there is total awareness and therefore it is best not to choose anywhere that you may be distracted. Distractions can include noise from traffic, noise from a television or radio, bright lights, the telephone ringing and so on. Some people are able to ignore such distractions better than others and it is up to you to judge for yourself whether an environment is suitable or not. As you become more adept at meditation, your ability to ignore such distractions will probably increase and indeed many people develop the ability to meditate successfully whilst sitting at their desk in the office, in a dentist's waiting room, on a bus or train or in a launderette. However, when starting out, it is best to choose a quiet, distraction-free environment, so make sure that the answering machine is on and choose a time of day when visitors are less likely to drop by.

There are no rules when it comes to meditation although may people find it helpful to develop a routine. The benefit of incorporating meditation into the daily routine has already been mentioned. It can also be useful to select a particular place to meditate as then this place will become associated with relaxation and will thus aid the meditation, much in the same way that we associate sleeping with our bedroom. Various other aids can be used to enhance the meditative experience and help to create the correct ambience but we shall look at this in more depth later on.

Duration

It is best to meditate at least once a day as it is harder to get back into after a break. Not only should you choose a time when you are less likely to be disturbed but you should also refrain from meditating straight away after a heavy meal. Also if alcohol has been consumed then the meditation will be less successful.

Although it is sometime helpful to set aside a particular time of the day to meditate, it is not completely necessary. The joy of meditation is that it can be done virtually anywhere and at any time. It is free of charge and requires no special clothes, accessories or equipment. It is up to you to discover what suits you best.

Neither is it necessary to meditate for a particular amount of time – the quality of the meditation is far more important than the duration. As a rough guide, you can aim to meditate between 15 to 30 minutes in the one sitting. As you become more practised at meditation, this can be increased, but a beginner would probably begin to feel discomfort after 30 minutes. When you start meditating regularly, you will become more efficient at judging how much time has elapsed and will no longer need to keep glancing at your watch. Some people prefer to meditate at night as the deep state of relaxation helps them to drift off to sleep afterwards, whereas others find that it has the opposite effect and so prefer to meditate first thing in the morning. If meditating more than once a day, it can be useful to separate meditations by a few hours, thus ensuring that your body and mind have a chance to recoup their energy. Once this time is up, you should sit for a couple of minutes and gradually become aware of your external surroundings again. Try to hang onto the feeling of relaxation as you go back to your day-to-day activities. The more you can introduce meditation into your daily life, the more beneficial it will be.

Factors which can prevent successful Meditation

The factors we have just discussed are all necessary if you want to meditate successfully. However, we are not quite ready to begin yet. As well as considering which factors are necessary to promote successful meditation, it is also necessary to be aware of those factors that can inhibit our ability to meditate.

Discomfort

It is much easier to meditate when the body is relaxed and comfortable but it is sometimes difficult to find a comfortable position. Physical discomfort is often related to mental anxiety. Sometimes when we try to sleep and our mind is preoccupied with some problem or other we imagine that we are unable to sleep due to not being able to find a comfortable position in bed. We toss and turn in a futile fashion, failing to realise that if we simply resolved the mental conflict we are suffering from then physical comfort would come automatically. The best way to deal with this is to ask yourself what it is that is worrying you. If you can pinpoint the problem, you can then attempt to resolve it and it will no longer hinder your attempts to meditate.

You can try various other methods to achieve physical comfort. One method is to start at the bottom of the body and tense and relax each muscle group. There is more detailed information on this as a relaxation technique in chapter 6. This can be used before you begin to meditate in order to relax the body.

You can also try a breathing exercise, as this is one of the most effective ways to relax the body and ease discomfort. Try to visualise the tension leaving your body with each exhalation of stale air.

If you are feeling uncomfortable, then try this exercise. Sit upright in a straight-backed chair. Begin to take deep, slow breaths, breathing deep into the lungs every time you inhale. Now feel all the tension that has become accumulated in your upper body. Now feel all the tension sinking down through your body, coming from every area including the arms, the neck, the chest, and all along the spine. Feel it all gather together at the bottom of your spine and feel the weight of it pulling you down into the chair. Now feel it vanishing out of your body, leaving you feeling relaxed and free of all tension.

If you are still feeling physical discomfort, then it is perhaps a good idea to change position. For example, if sitting in a straight-backed chair is uncomfortable for you, you could try sitting back in a recliner, or even lying on the floor. Be careful not to become too comfortable though, as you do not want to risk falling asleep. It is more difficult to maintain an alert mind when lying down, but not impossible. As long as you are aware of the danger of dozing off then you should be able to prevent it.

Sometimes, if the physical discomfort is only mild, it is a good idea to simply acknowledge it as a sensation like any other before drawing your attention back to the meditation. This is a similar method to the one we employ when stray thoughts emerge in our consciousness and threaten to distract us from the object of our meditation. Whenever your mind turns to contemplate the pain you are suffering, remain passive to that thought and redirect your consciousness back to the meditation. Try this method, and you may even find that your physical discomfort disappears.

An Over-Active Mind

Sometimes when you attempt to meditate, your mind will be more active that usual and you will find that you are constantly interrupted by random thoughts flowing through your mind. This can happens for any number of reasons. For example, you could be having a particularly hectic day, you may be preoccupied with something that is worrying you, you may just have received some exciting news or you could be looking forward to something happening later in the day. Your mind is used to flitting from one thought to another without us trying to control it so when you try to put a rein on your thoughts, it is natural that you should find this difficult.

Allowing your mind to wander in this way is a long-established habit, and as anyone who has tried to kick a long-term habit knows, this can be very difficult to break. However, an over-active mind is always going to hinder successful meditation. If your mind is constantly jumping from one thought to another, you will never achieve the level of concentration necessary in raising your sense of awareness in order to perceive the reality of existence – one of the primary goals of meditation. So, if you are committed to learning to meditate, then an excited mind is something you must learn to control.

There are several ways you can overcome an overactive mind. One method you can use is to concentrate on the natural rhythm of your breathing. Whenever your mind wanders, simply draw it back to the rhythm of your breathing. Do this for a few minutes and your mental excitement should eventually subside. This is very similar to the breathing meditations we will look at in the next chapter but a quicker version to be used as a prelude to a full meditation. Once your mind is more calm you can begin to meditate.

If you continually suffer from an over-active mind then it might be to change the position you are meditating in to one that you find more comfortable. You should also make sure that you are correctly using the position that you have chosen. If the neck is craned then this in itself can produce an over-active mind, so check that your posture is straight, you head is facing directly ahead and you are stable and comfortable.

Remember to remain patient at all times. If you try too hard to calm your mind it will simply have the opposite effect and you will become stressed. Do not become annoyed with yourself or disappointed if this does not seem to work straightaway. Just keep attempting to calm your mind and, over time with regular practise, this will become much easier.

Sleepiness

While sleepiness is the opposite of the previous problem, it is no less disruptive when attempting to meditate. Sleepiness can manifest itself in varying degrees from slight lethargy to the point where you are actually dozing off during meditation. This can happen when you first begin to meditate as the brain is used to going to sleep when you relax and close your eyes.

As with an over-active mind, sleepiness can be caused by an incorrect posture, so ensure that your spine is straight and you head is facing directly in front of you. Although meditating is usually practised with the eyes closed, when you are feeling sleepy then it is all right to meditate with them open. Also, check that you are not too warm. If you are, then remove a layer of clothing. You can also check that there is enough fresh air in the room and if not, then open a window.

Sleepiness or lethargy can also be caused by an underlying problem such as an intensely stressful lifestyle or depression. If you suspect that this is the case then it is best to get to the root of the problem. Depression can be treated by practising one of the meditations in chapter 11 of this book. For example, the meditation on mortality is said to be an effective meditation for those who are feeling depressed.

If you are still finding it hard to overcome your

sleepiness then it may be that you are just physically tired. If this is the case then try taking a nap or just taking a break from meditating and try again later. For those of you who suffer frequently from fatigue, it is perhaps more effective to meditate in the morning when you have just woken up, as this is when we tend to be most alert.

A Negative Attitude

Successful meditation is often prevented by an individual's belief that he or she will never be able to master it. Some people give up after one or two attempts, and others stick with it for longer but feel as though they have not improved at all. This is because, a negative attitude can hinder the individuals attempts to meditate. You may be so busy looking for results that you do not fully involve yourself in the meditation. Alternatively, you can be so determined to meditate successful that you are repeatedly trying too hard and preventing yourself from fully relaxing. The secret is to try to avoid having too high expectations and then you will neither be disappointed if these are not fulfilled, nor will you strive too hard.

Try to maintain a realistic and laid-back approach. Meditation goes against several habits that we have probably been practising for most of our lives, so it is inevitable that you will find it tricky to begin with. Some people find that the benefits of meditation can appear almost immediately and others find that it takes much longer. It really depends on the individual, so do not worry if it seems to be taking a while for you.

While meditation can have a remarkably positive effect on your life and can lead to major changes in your lifestyle, do not expect this to happen straightaway. It is important that you remain patient. Think of taking up meditation as a long-term part of your lifestyle, similar to changing your diet, and do not be too eager to change. This will happen inevitably as you become more self-aware and start to scrutinise your old way of life, but it will be a gradual process of change, not a sudden one. Try to enjoy each meditation for its own sake – think of it as a time when you can completely relax and momentarily escape the stress of life. If you enjoy each and every meditation, then you will be happy to continue whether you are aware of any results or not and when you stop looking for them is the time when they are most likely to appear.

It is important that if you are suffering from one of the above things that you take a little time to try to alleviate your symptoms before you attempt to meditate. First time meditations can seem tricky enough without having added difficulties to overcome. Once you have worked out what the problem is and managed to resolve it, you are ready to begin.

CHAPTER 7
The Importance of Breathing

We have already stated the basic conditions necessary when practising meditation, and correct breathing has to be one of the most important. Breathing correctly by breathing deep into the lungs in a rhythmic fashion is not only essential when relaxing during meditation but, as we have just discussed, it is also an ideal focus when meditating. Breathing is used as a focus by most of the traditional schools of meditation such as Buddhism and Taoism.

Breathing can be considered an effective focus on which to meditate for several reasons. We have already discussed the relaxing effects of breathing and will expand upon this in the next chapter. Using breathing to concentrate on while meditating, produces all the benefits of meditating that we have already discussed such as greater levels of energy, a feeling of peace and contentment, a more stable nervous system, improved concentration, improved efficiency and increased creativity.

Breathing both reflects and has an effect on our state of body and mind. Of course, when we exert ourselves in any way, our breathing becomes quicker to allow the transportation of larger amounts of oxygen to vital organs. However, when we are excited, our breaths become also quick, shallow and irregular as though we are preparing subconsciously for a 'fight or flight' reaction or a moment of great exertion. When we are very relaxed, we take deeper, slower and more rhythmical breaths. When we are in suspense, we sometimes hold our breath altogether as though we are attempting to suspend our lives until a particular moment of tension is over. Alternatively, if we are agitated and excited, our first reaction can often be an attempt to try and control our emotions by controlling our breath. If we force ourselves to take deep, slow rhythmical breaths then often our minds and body automatically become more relaxed. This interrelationship between breathing and state of mind has long been recognised and it is hardly surprising that many people realised that they could consciously utilise this relationship to improve the state of physical and mental health.

Using breathing as the main focus during meditation can promote a state of deep relaxation both mentally and physically. Therefore, it is one of the most effective types of meditation for those whose main objective is the release of stress through meditation. Simply concentrating on the abdominal movements during breathing can lead to a high level of relaxation, removing muscle tension whilst simultaneously quietening the stream of thoughts in the mind. It can also help to introduce and maintain calm in an overactive nervous system. As the meditation proceeds, you will no longer feel that you are breathing of your own volition but will only feel the sensation itself.

Using breathing as a stimulus is an excellent exercise for beginners and for experts in meditation. Because it is a simple process that we are never without, it will not seem too new or unusual for someone coming to meditation for the first time. For those who are better practised in meditation, using a breathing-focused meditation is still an excellent discipline and can lead to the highest levels of relaxation. Using your own breathing as the focus for your meditation is also cheap, easy and convenient, as it is free of charge, can be taken anywhere and can be utilised at any time.

Focussing on breathing also keep us in touch with our greatest life force, whilst reminding us of our own mortality – we require oxygen more than any other substance to say alive. However, while breathing is an involuntary action – something we do without thinking about it, as opposed to eating or drinking – we are able to manipulate and control our breathing to some degree and this is what we are doing during meditation. Becoming more aware of our own breathing can also be beneficial to the health as we often take shallow breaths and fail to fill our lungs to their full capacity. Becoming accustomed to taking slower, deeper and more rhythmic breaths will improve our breathing during everyday life, supplying more oxygen to the body, thus making our bodies more productive whilst promoting alertness and preventing lethargy.

During a meditation on the breathing, our attention is directed towards the breathing process. This is an internal process and difficult to visualise, so many forms of meditation choose to focus on one particular part of the body involved in that process. For example, some people choose to focus on the tip of the nose as the point above where the air is inhaled. This is an effective point of focus as it is possible the feel the coolness of the air passing through the nose into the lungs. Others choose to focus on the abdomen when meditating as when we breathe, the abdomen naturally rises and falls in a rhythmical fashion.

You will find that during the meditation that your attention will wander from the focus of your meditation – your inhalations and exhalations. This is inevitable and happens to everyone during meditation, including those people who are highly proficient. The important thing is not to become frustrated and angry with yourself, but simply acknowledge that your attention has wandered and then calmly redirect it back to focussing on your breathing.

While focusing on breathing is highly effective for the beginner, you may want to explore other methods of meditation as you become more advanced. Do not think, however, that this a basic form of meditation to be discarded in favour of more complicated techniques. You can continue to use it on its own or as a preface to other forms of meditation as is an excellent way of priming the mind and body for meditation as well as being a highly effective method in itself.

When using breathing as a focus for meditation, there are two methods you can use. Firstly, you can deliberately manipulate your breathing in order to relax as we have previously discussed. Perhaps the purer method though is to simply be aware of the breathing process itself without consciously trying to manipulate it. As you concentrate on the rhythms of your breathing, you will find that the breathing becomes regular and smooth of its own accord without you having to consciously strive to achieve this. So, both of these methods actually produce the same end result – that is regular, even, correct breathing.

As we have mentioned, breathing-focused meditation is an effective form of meditation and can be used alone both by the beginner and those who are more advanced at meditation. When using the breathing as a lead-in to another meditation, it is only necessary to practise it for five to ten minutes. By this time, the body and mind will be sufficiently relaxed and more receptive to alternative forms of meditation.

Now we have covered the basic rules of posture and technique, we can begin with a simple meditation on the breath.

BASIC BREATHING EXERCISE NO 1
* Firstly, find a suitable environment for meditating. Choose somewhere quiet and peaceful where you

are unlikely to be disturbed.

- As with any meditation, select a position that feels comfortable and where you remain stable with a straight spine and the head facing straight-ahead. Choose one of the positions from chapter 4 or introduce one of your own.
- Eyes should remain shut. Take deep, slow breaths following a regular rhythm.
- Keep your attention focused on your breathing. You can do this in many ways. You can choose to focus on the rhythm of your breathing, or concentrate your attention first on exhaling and inhaling. Alternatively, focus on the feeling of the air passing through your nostrils or on the tip of your nose, or the rising and falling of the diaphragm as you breathe.
- Count for five and then exhale slowly. Repeat this five to ten times. Now, begin to breathe at a normal speed, but inhale slightly deeper than you would normally. Keep breathing normally, focusing all the time on the rhythm of your breathing. The deeper into the meditation you go, the more regular and rhythmic your breathing will become.
- You will find that distracting thoughts will begin to flit through your mind. When this happens simply acknowledge them then turn your attention back to focusing on your breathing. Try to remain relaxed and calm at all times.
- Practice this exercise a few times or until you feel ready to move on. Remember that an exercise that

you feel is doing you good is worth continuing with. However, if you come across one that you do not enjoy, or which makes you feel uncomfortable, then stop immediately as it can have little positive effect.

Breathing meditations such as this one are perfect for the beginner as they are easy to master and require no complicated props or mantras. They are also one of the most effective forms of meditation. In the following chapter, we will discuss the way in which you can combine this awareness of your own breathing with the powers of your imagination to achieve even greater levels of relaxation, but for the moment we shall look at some more breathing meditations.

Counting Each Breath

You can also meditate on your own breathing by counting each breath. Try this simple exercise.

BASIC BREATHING EXERCISE NO 2
- Again, find a suitable environment for meditating.
- Adopt the position that you find comfortable. You can use the same position that you used in the last exercise if you wish.
- Close your eyes and begin to breathe deeply and slowly. Breathe through the nostrils and deep into the lungs.
- Again, keep your attention focused on your

breathing. Remember that you can focus on the rhythm of your breathing, concentrate your attention first on exhaling and inhaling, focus on the feeling of the air passing through your nostrils, focus on the tip of your nose, or focus on the rising and falling of the diaphragm as you breathe.

- Now start counting every time you inhale. Start at one and when you reach ten, begin again. Continue like this for the rest of the meditation.

- Again, you will probably find that you are distracted from the focus of your attention with stray thoughts. When this happens just acknowledge them then turn your attention back to counting your exhalations, beginning the counting from 'one' again. Remember to remain relaxed and calm at all times.

- Practice this exercise for a few minutes and then end the meditation by becoming slowly aware of your surroundings again.

This is also a popular exercise in meditation for a beginner. In this exercise, we count the breaths as a way of helping us to focus on breathing. It is best to count up to ten and then start again at the beginning, as counting to a higher number requires more concentration. You can count at any part of the breathing cycle, whether on the inhalation, the exhalation or the slight pause in between. Counting not only draws more attention to the object we are focussing on, but also provides a relatively simple way of preventing the attention from wandering too far from the object. If we break from counting, we soon become aware of this and direct our attention back to our stimulus.

The most effective way to count is inside your head. Thus, you do not break the silence of the meditation or potentially distract yourself from the meditation by the effort of forming speech. You can count when you inhale, exhale, or on the slight pause in between, but it is most common to count as you exhale. This is because when you exhale the stale air this can be viewed as the completion of the process of imbibing air and extracting the oxygen from it, before exhaling the toxins produced by the body along with the spent air. You should only count to ten before starting from one again because, as I mentioned before, it is very difficult to maintain concentrate if you exceed ten when counting.

In chapter 4, we mentioned briefly the most effective way of breathing. This is when you take slow, even breaths that fill the lungs almost to their fullest capacity. If your breaths are too shallow, this will become obvious, as the movements that occur in your abdomen as you breathe will become less pronounced. It is important to ensure that you are breathing correctly, as overly shallow, irregular breathing will not have the same relaxing effects as proper breathing. For more information on breathing, see chapters 3 and 4.

You may feel that the exercise of counting the breaths is simplistic and easy to achieve but once you have attempted it, you will see how difficult it can be too keep the mind focussed on one activity. Your mind will inevitably wander off, but this is no bad thing, as all sorts of valuable thoughts can come to us in this way. The main thing to remember is that when the mind wanders off simply redirect it to the counting of the breaths, beginning again from one. Most importantly, do not try too hard, as the mere effort of preventing these thoughts from entering the brain just increases the chance of them doing that very thing. Also, to exert too much effort on concentrating will prevent you from becoming fully relaxed and will therefore hinder the meditative process. Accept that these thoughts are a natural function of the mind and they will not prove to be too much of a disruption. Remember to use a particular area of the abdomen to focus on when counting the breaths and this will help you to remain alert and focussed.

Meditating on the Breath/Mindfulness of Breath

Once you have mastered meditation where you count each breath you are ready to move onto a meditation where you remain aware of your breathing but no longer count each breath. This is what the Buddhists refer to as 'mindfulness of breathing'. Breathing should be allowed to flow following a natural rhythm and the mind's focus should remain on the breathing itself. This meditation can also be done on its own, or can follow a breathing meditation where you count each breath, or can act as a precursor to another meditation. These exercises are flexible and it is up to you as an individual to decide which meditations or combinations of meditations you prefer.

As you become more advanced at meditation, you will develop the concentration necessary to simply be aware of the breathing process itself rather than focussing on one part of it or counting each breath. You can just be aware of it as a cyclical process rather than a number of automated actions. However, at any stage in your development, you can go back to counting as an affective way of re-focusing the attention and counting the breaths is an effective way to lead into a meditation on the breath itself.

Try the following exercise.

BASIC BREATHING EXERCISE NO 3
- Again, choose a suitable environment for meditating. By this time you should begin to have an idea of what works best for you.
- Adopt the position that you have chosen as the most comfortable for you or, if you like, experiment with a new position. Remain upright, stationary and in a comfortable and stable position.
- Close your eyes and begin to breathe deeply and slowly at a regular pace. Breathe through the nostrils and deep down into the lungs.
- Keep your attention focused on your breathing but this time do not count the individual breaths but consider the breathing as a cyclical process. Focus

on the rhythm of your breathing, as you inhale, hold for a slight pause and then exhale the stale air. Focus on the feeling of the air passing through your nostrils, the tip of your nose. Feel the way that the abdomen first rises as you inhale and then falls as you exhale.

- Try not to regulate the breathing – this may sound simple but it tempting to start trying to control the depth and duration of each breath. Try not to judge each breath but simply be aware of it and after a while the breathing will become regular and relaxed and the consciousness will go deeper and deeper into the meditation.

- As always, you will find that distracting thoughts will begin to flit through your mind – perhaps even more so as this is a new technique. When this happens simply acknowledge these thoughts, then turn your attention back to the sensation of your breathing. Try to remain relaxed and calm at all times. Do not focus on your role in producing these breaths but think of the breathing something that is happening to your body.

- Practise this exercise as often as you feel is necessary to master it and remember not to strive to hard to achieve mindfulness as this effort itself can hinder meditation.

Other Breathing Techniques used in Meditation

Ujjayi Breath

The Ujjayi Breath is achieved when you partially close the epiglottis at the back of your throat. When you do this it means that your breathing becomes slightly restricted and it makes a sort of hissing sound. Many people breathe this way when they are sleeping. If you are practising this technique, do not force your breath thus making a loud, rasping noise. The breath should be allowed to pass through the airways gradually and the sound produced should be a gentle, quiet sound. By producing this sound, this form of breathing can help your concentration as you can focus your attention on the sound that it produces. This breathing technique can also be incorporated into any meditation.

Creating Tension in the Tanden Centre

This is a slightly more difficult form of breathing to achieve. The Tanden Centre is the name that Zen Buddhists give to the centre of spiritual power that they believe to be in the diaphragm. To create this feeling of tension, all that you do is to manipulate the diaphragm and abdomen. Normally when you breathe, your diaphragm contracts when you inhale and then it relaxes again when you exhale and your abdominal muscles are used to empty air out of the lungs. To create this tension, you force the diaphragm to work harder while resisting with the abdominal muscles and then when you exhale, your abdominal muscles are forced to work harder whilst your diaphragm supplies resistance. In this way, neither the diaphragm nor the abdominal muscles ever completely relax but are always tensed to some degree. By maintaining the feeling of tension in this way, you are creating focus that is effective in stopping the mind wandering. Many who have mastered this technique also claim that there are other benefits to doing so.

For more information on breathing techniques, see the yoga section in chapter 14.

CHAPTER 8
The Importance of Relaxation

In order to meditate successfully, it is important that you learn to relax properly. This is area worth spending time on to promote the beneficial effects of meditation, particularly if you are someone who finds it difficult to fully relax. When attempting to relax, we should pay attention to two areas. Firstly, we must learn to relax mentally. This involves slowing the rapid stream of thoughts that flow through our minds. The second stage in relaxation is to reduce the physical tension in our bodies. You will find that working on one has an affect on the other as the two are mutually dependent. This also means that if you neglect the mind when relaxing, it will hinder your attempts to relax your body and vice versa.

It can be very difficult to learn to relax as the effort itself can hinder true relaxation. It is therefore best not to try too hard and instead just allow the feelings of relaxation to wash over you. It is important to proceed with a positive mental attitude. If you doubt your ability to relax before you have even begun then it is unlikely that you will succeed. If on the other hand you attempt to quash any doubts and go in with the attitude that you will succeed, then you are far more likely to.

A Meditation Exercise to Relax the Mind

An effective way of slowing down the mind is instead of trying to create a dam to block out the stream of thoughts that flow in and out of our consciousness, we should instead allow each thought to fully realise itself. Acknowledge each thought, one after the other. Allow this process to continue for as long as you feel necessary. This method is successful as the consciousness does not try and fight the unconsciousness and in its struggle for supremacy creating internal turmoil before inevitable failure. Instead, it allows the two forces to work in harmony therefore creating a focussed and tranquil mind.

A Meditation Exercise to Relax the Body

Once you feel you have calmed the mind sufficiently, you are ready to work on the body.

Assume the position that you have decided is most comfortable for you and close your eyes. Start taking deep breaths - a little deeper than you would breath normally. Focus your attention on the oxygen filling your lungs. With each inhalation, imagine the oxygen as a positive life-giving force. Picture the oxygen as it diffuses into the blood stream. Now imagine the oxygen as it is transported to each area of the body in turn and carried away are the waste products of the body and also the tension. With each exhalation, picture the toxins that you are emitting with the spent oxygen. As you exhale, feel the tension also flow out of your body. Let your exhalations transport the tension far away, allowing you to fully relax.

Using the imagination this way has a great effect on the body. Imagining a feeling of relaxation sweeping over the body in this way and aiding your imagination with pictorial content can actually help your body relax. It also increases your awareness of the different areas of your body, ensuring that no part is left tense. Imagining what is feels like to relax will result in the body actually relaxing – this shows the power of positive thought and also the extent to which the body and the mind are co-dependent.

Physical Exercise

As well as using the power of the mind to relax both body and mind, it is also worth considering physical exercise. This is one of the best ways of releasing tension so it is a good idea to visit your local leisure centre to find out what facilities are available. Do not worry if you are not physically fit - it does not have to be strenuous. Even a gentle walk in the park can release tension.

For those for whom mobility is a problem, there are alternatives. Another effective way to release tension is the simple procedure of using stretching and tensing exercises.

See also chapter 14, which has details of the Alexander Technique and yoga, two practices that can be used in conjunction with meditation to aid relaxation. These are both excellent complementary practices to meditation and are worth exploring if you have the time.

Stretching Exercises

As a preface to meditation, try stretching every area of your body, focussing on the spine, limb, fingers and toes. It is probably most effective to try this lying down if possible.

Most people 'grow' at least an inch in height during the night due to the fact that the spine tends to contract due to both the force of gravity and to many people's tendency to slouch. This can be counteracted by stretching the spine as far as it will go. These stretching exercises are an excellent way of keeping muscles toned and supple without over-exertion and are therefore particularly suitable for people with people who are unfit, suffer from high blood pressure or have a disability of some sort.

It is important to be aware of any built-up tension in your body and to treat it before it has a permanent effect on your health and posture.

A Meditation Exercise to Aid Stretching

Take up a suitable position for meditating and close your eyes. Imagine your spine curled and contracted. Now imagine it beginning to uncurl and stretch to its longest length – visualise each vertebra becoming longer in length. As you imagine this, feel your actual spine stretching and your lung cavities increasing in capacity.

Tensing Exercises

Odd as it may sound, tensing the muscles may actually get rid of feeling off tension. If the muscles are tensed and then relaxed, the contrast between the two states enhances the eventual feeling of relaxation.

Try the following exercise:

- Close your eyes. Focus your attention on your inner self. Acknowledge each thought before letting it go to make way for the next. Take deep breaths, relax and let go of any inhibitions.
- Let your mind focus on your feet. Slowly circle them around at the ankle and feel the joints start to loosen. Contract the muscles of the feet as tight as you can. Hold that for five seconds, concentrating on the feeling of tension the entire time. Now release all the feeling of tensions. Let them go. Feel the muscles relaxing, becoming loose and heavy. Feel the sense of release. Feel the relief that this brings.

- Now, turn your mind to the calves. Contract the muscles and hold your five seconds. Concentrate on the feeling of tension that you are experiencing – it is real and palpable. If at all helpful, try and visualise the muscles in their contracted state. Now release the tension. Feel it seeping out of your calves. Feel your muscles become soft and supple once more. Enjoy the feeling that comes with the release of tension.

- Move up the legs to the thighs. Contract the thigh muscles, hold for five seconds and then release the tension. Feel the increased feeling of relaxation as it travels up your body.

- Now onto the buttocks. Contract the muscles as tightly as you can, hold for five seconds and then let go.

- Now move up to the abdomen. Contract the muscles as tightly as you can, hold for five seconds and then let go. Concentrate on the feelings of relaxation that should now be travelling up your body, eliminating all feelings of pent-up tension.

- Now move your attention to the chest. Contract the chest muscles, inhaling deeply at the same time. Hold this position for five seconds and then exhale, feeling all the tension dispel from that area.

- Now travel further up the body to concentrate on the arms. Contract your muscles all the way down the arms and into the hands and clench your fists. Hold this for five seconds and then let go. By now you should be feeling the deep sense of relaxation travelling up through your body. Hold onto that feeling and enjoy it.

- Now, move up to the shoulders. Contract the shoulder muscles, hold for five seconds and then let go. You can also try circling them backwards and forwards to loosen them up even more. Feel the tension dispel, firstly from between the shoulder blades, and then from the neck and the surrounding area.

- Finally, turn your attention to the face. Tense up all the facial muscles. It may help to contort you features to make sure you exercise each one. And now relax these muscles again.

- By now you should feel the waves of relaxation sweeping through you – your body should be relaxed and your mind should be calm and tranquil.

Background Music to Aid Relaxation

Many people assume that they require complete silence in order to mediate properly, that noise of any sort will prove to be a distracting influence. However this is completely untrue. Background noise can in fact promote relaxation, provided that it does not distract you from the task at hand.

Different types of noise work for different people. Visit any new age shop and there is a vast selection of tapes that are specifically designed to aid relaxation such as bird song or chiming. You may find music relaxing, such as classical, pan pipes, baroque or choral. To find out what works best for you, it is useful to experiment with various types of background noise. Try selecting a number of different tapes and after each meditation take note of the effect that a particular sound had on you.

Relaxation through Aromatherapy

Another alternative therapy that can be used to promote relaxation is aromatherapy. Aromatherapy is the practice of treating certain conditions by way of the olfactory senses, and like meditation, it is a practice that has been in use for thousands of years. Aromatherapy uses essential oils, which are oils obtained from plants and flowers. They are quite expensive to produce as it can take a great many plants to obtain just a few drops of oil. For example, it would require 6 tonnes of orange blossom to produce 1 kg of neroli oil.

Aromatherapy oils are usually used by mixing them with carrier oils and then massaging them into the body. It is also possible to benefit from aromatherapy oils, by placing them in an oil burner and allowing their aroma to fill the room. To aid your meditations, try burning some oil in the room while you meditate, or perhaps go for an aromatherapy massage prior to your meditative session.

The following oils are particularly good for relaxation.

- *Cedarwood*: This oil has a dry perfume with wood tones. It is effective for soothing and focusing a distracted mind.

- *Chamomile*: This oil has a mild aroma. It is renowned for its soothing properties and is particularly good for preventing insomnia. It also has a calming effect on the mind, body and emotions.

- *Clary Sage*: This oil has a nutty fragrance. It is effective at counteracting depression and has a rejuvenating effect. It is also said to be deeply relaxing.

- *Frankincense*: This oil has a resinous fragrance. It is said to be particularly good for use in conjunction with meditation and is also believed to soothe and strengthen the mind.

- *Geranium*: This oil has a floral aroma. It is believed to be a particularly relaxing oil and soothes the mind and body, whilst helping to balance the emotions.

- *Lavender*: This oil also has a flowery fragrance and is also said to be particularly good for relaxing the mind and body.

- *Lemon*: This has a fresh, lemon fragrance. It is said to be good for bringing clarity to the mind and the emotions.

- *Marjoram*: This oil has a warm and spicy smell. It is supposed to be good for relaxing the muscles and preventing insomnia.

- *Patchouli*: This oil has a musky fragrance. It is

effective in uplifting the spirit whilst imbuing the mind with a greater sense of clarity.

- *Sandalwood*: This oil has a sweet aroma with wood tones. It is said to soothe both the body and the mind.
- *Ylang Ylang*: This oil has a sweet, floral fragrance. It is renowned for its relaxing properties and is said to regulate the nerves.

Muscle Relaxation

We have already considered the power of mind over matter and explored the co-dependency of the body and mind. We shall now take this one step further and actually relax muscle groups simply by making a mental suggestion to each muscle group.

Meditation to Relax the Muscles

- Assume a comfortable position and close the eyes.
- Take slow, deep breaths, filling the lungs to their fullest capacity.
- Whether sitting or lying, feel the force of gravity pull you down. Your body is loose and heavy.
- Continue breathing slowly and deeply.
- Start to feel the tension throughout your body dispel, slowly and steadily.
- Continue breathing slowly and deeply. Feel all the tension leaving your body with each exhalation.
- Now starting at the bottom of the body and,

working your way up, visualise each part of the body becoming relaxed. Imagine what this feels like.

- Concentrate on your feet. Feel the tension leave them. Your feet feel completely relaxed.
- Move to the ankles. Imagine all the built up tension start to lessen. Your ankles feel completely relaxed.
- Now imagine the tension in your calves. Feel that tension and then feel it slip away, leaving the muscles loose and supple.
- Now focus on your knees. Feel the tension leave your knees. Your knees feel completely relaxed.
- Moving up your body to focus on the thighs. Your thighs feel completely relaxed.
- Now up to your buttocks. Feel the tension vanish. Your buttocks feel completely relaxed.
- By now the entire bottom half of your body feels completely relaxed. Hold onto that feeling that tension is leaving our body.
- Now move up to your abdomen. Feel the tension vanish. Your abdomen feels completely relaxed.
- Feel the relaxation sweep up your body as the tension slips away.
- Focus on your chest. Your chest feels completely relaxed.
- Continue to breathe slowly and deeply, feeling the tension leave your body with each exhalation.
- Now feel a sense of relaxation all the way down your arms into your hands. Visualise the tension seep out the body through the fingertips.

- The entire body from the neck down is now completely relaxed.
- Continue to take deep slow breaths, in and out. With each exhalation more and more tension leaves the body.
- Now feel a deep sense of relaxation travel even further up your body, up through the neck and into the face.
- The muscles in your face feel completely relaxed.
- Continue to take deep, slow breaths.
- Feel the waves of relaxation now sweep over your entire body.
- All tension has now left your body and your mind is serene and tranquil.
- Hold that feeling for a few minutes before gradually becoming aware of your external surroundings and opening you eyes. You should now be fully relaxed both physically and mentally.

CHAPTER 9
Exploring the Power of Thought in Meditation

One of the main benefits of meditation is the way in which it can bring a deep sense of tranquillity to the mind, slowing down the constant stream of thoughts that we all receive and instilling a sense of calm and focus. Most of us at some point have suffered from late night anxiety attacks and it is easy to lose sense of perspective on a problem or negative thought that we have been dwelling on.

Many people also find that the constant presence and speed of their thoughts leaves them dizzy. They can never hold on to one though for more than a couple of seconds before a new thought comes to replace it and in order to think clearly and rationally about matters at hand, it is necessary to first cut through this white noise. Such disorganisation in the mind can soon lead to disorganisation in day-to-day life, as this lack of focus leads to forgetfulness and confusion in general. However, meditation can have a positive effect on our thoughts in other ways, too. We have briefly look at the potential power of thought and we will now consider this at greater length.

Negative Thought Patterns

The power of thought is often underestimated. Our thoughts can have a huge part in determining the course that our lives will take. If we have negative thought patterns then we can be prone to failure, as believing that you will never succeed at something is often enough to ensure that you never will. Then when the predicted failure happens, it is used to confirm what we suspected in the first place - that we were never any good in the first place. In other words, negative thought patterns can be a self-fulfilling prophecy.

We cannot underestimate the power that our thought patterns can have on our life. Negative thought patterns can be deeply ingrained without us even realising it. But meditation can turn this around. Just as negative thought has negative consequences, the power of positive thought can be enormous, too. However deeply instilled these negative thoughts are in our minds, mediation can help to take these apart and turn them into positive patterns of thought.

Stop to consider the thoughts that have gone through your mind most recently. Have any of these been negative? An example of a negative thought could be, 'I'm no good at fixing things; I don't have that kind of brain, or 'I will never manage to pass my exams – I'm just not capable of it.'

We all have set ideas of our strengths and weaknesses, which are sometimes accurate, but more often then not they are fallacious. Because we think we are a certain 'type' of person then we will never be good at certain types of task. These types of negative thought patterns mean that we are often defeated before we even begin, or can mean that we are discouraged from even trying in the first place. We also subconsciously give off this attitude to other people so that sometimes they can pick up on this and confirm our negative opinions to us. These negative thought patterns can cut us off from many interests that we might have enjoyed had we not been already convinced of our supposed shortcomings.

Thoughts are closely linked to what we class as our beliefs. Everyone has a set of beliefs that they apply to the world. These beliefs can sometimes be foolish but if you consider just how much information we receive from our environment that we have to then process, it is no wonder that we sometimes form a belief without having all the information. It is our way of simplifying the world and making it easier to understand.

In overcoming these negative thought patterns, it is said to be useful to make a list of all of your beliefs that spring to mind. First of all consider the way in which they affect your behaviour – this should give you and idea of how pervasive they are and how much influence they actually yield. Secondly, pick out those that you are most certain off and imagine that they are not true and that you in fact believe the opposite. This allows you to open you mind enough to question those beliefs that you hold dear, and also to consider how your behaviour, and your success rate at various tasks, may change if your beliefs were different.

Turning Negative Thoughts Around

Now that you are aware of your thoughts and beliefs, and the degree to which these affect your behaviour, you will be able to exert some conscious effort into changing your life for the better. This will allow you to alter thought and behaviour patterns where necessary, to make positive changes in your life, instead of just believing that things happen to you because of the kind of person that you believe yourself to be.

Meditation can aid you in pinpointing the negative thoughts and beliefs that may have been hindering you in your life and will give you the focus and drive to change them. Positive thought is such a simple solution that many people may be sceptical of its potential benefits but it IS possible for us to change the way we think – an act which can have positive and lasting benefit in our lives. If we concentrate on our weaknesses and past failures allowing these to spread their influence throughout our present and our future then we will continue to fail at our endeavours. However, if we simply tell ourselves that we can do something; that it is possible to succeed, then often this is enough to make us succeed.

Mantras

One method useful for encouraging positive thought it the repetition of a mantra while meditating. We have already looked at the use of mantras when considering the technique employed in Transcendental Meditation. While in TM the mantra is usually chosen for each person by his or her instructor, it is also common in meditation for each person to choose his or her own mantra. We will now investigate the use of mantras further. *The Oxford English Dictionary* (1995) defines **mantra** thus:

Mantra: *n.* **1a** a word or sound repeated to aid concentration in meditation, originally in Hinduism and Buddhism. **2a** Vedic Hymn. [Sanskrit, = instrument of thought, from man 'think']

Notice the etymology of the word – it originates from the Sanskrit word for 'think'. This serves to underline both the source and the target of the mantra – our thoughts. While the dictionary classes 'a word or sound' as a mantra, it is probably more useful if we broaden this to include any phrase or sentence that we wish to use.

It is useful if you decide upon a mantra for yourself, choosing a negative thought that you are prone to and counteracting it with a positive one. Once decided upon, the mantra should be repeated over and over again. This allows the mind to focus entirely on the phrase and what it means to you, simultaneously ridding itself of any distracting or negative thoughts.

If you cannot think of one, here are some suggestions of general mantras that can be applied to most people's lives:

- Life is an interesting and challenging journey.

- I am shaping my destiny.

- I feel content and tranquil.

- I shall take pleasure in the here and now.

- Anything can be achieved.

- I feel stronger every day.

- I am filled with health and vitality.

- I take control of my life.

- I shall make my dreams come true.

- I can change that which I do not like about myself.

- I know and love myself.

- Whatever goals I have will be achieved.

- My confidence increases every day.

- I feel love and good will towards my family.

- I feel love and good will towards my enemies.

- I feel love and good will towards myself.

- I can cope with every situation.

Meditating Using Mantras

- Assume a comfortable position and close your eyes.
- Compose a mantra or chose one of the ones from the above list.
- Take deeps breaths. If you are feeling tense, use the tensing muscles exercise or the mind-suggestion meditation in order to relax.
- When you are prepared, begin to repeat your mantra slowly, over and over again. Consider the meaning of the words and feel the positive meaning replace the negative one.
- Repeat for a few minutes, then gradually become aware of your external surroundings and open your eyes.

Changing Set Patterns of Behaviour

It is not only possible to target individual thoughts when meditating as we also alter entire patterns of behaviour. This can be used in various situations and is particularly useful in combating nervousness and increasing self-confidence. Many people suffer anxiety in certain situations. This can range from the common problem of suffering nerves when having to speak in public to the more rare and distressing anxiety that an agoraphobic suffers when stepping outside. Mediation can be used as a tool to increase you self-confidence by working on it from within.

First of all, define the part of your mind-set or behaviour that you wish to change. Let's say, for example, that you wish to increase your confidence when giving a presentation to a room full of strangers. Pinpoint exactly which parts of the experience fill you with dread. Identify those negative thoughts that have turned a relatively simple task into an anxiety-inducing situation.

You may feel that you will fail to convince your intended audience or that you may be heckled. You may have had a bad experience in the past. Identify the root of your fears and the influence of past events on present thoughts. You may be reacting in a way that was appropriate in the past but that is no longer and appropriate reaction. You may simply be experiencing a fear of fear itself, as you have learned to associate this situation with fear, are used to feeling fear when placed in this situation and are scared that you will become overcome with fear when you next attempt it. This can be a vicious circle, but it is a circle that can be broken with a little positive thought.

While it is difficult to change our feelings, particularly ones as strong and compelling as fear and anxiety, it is possible to change our thoughts - the source of our feelings. While meditating, think of a mantra to counteract your particular fear. Repeating this over and over will help to re-programme your mindset, thus breaking the link between the action which you fear and your reaction of fear. Your new reaction will instead be one of relaxation, confidence and positive feelings. Another powerful tool for replacing negative thought with more positive ones is imagery and we shall look at this in more depth in the next chapter. Try visualising yourself in the situation that you fear. Imagine yourself to be relaxed, confident and fully in control of the situation. Imagine a problem arising and watch the more confident you handling it, perhaps making a joke out of it, and then moving back the task at hand.

CHAPTER 10

Meditation Using Visual Imagery

We have already discussed the importance of having some kind of stimulus on which to focus on during meditation in order to keep the mind alert. As I mentioned in the last chapter, visualisation, or mental imagery can be an enormously powerful aid to meditation. In fact, visual images are always present in our thought processes. Try following your stream of conscious and observe how easily a thought can spark off a particular image or vice versa.

When we use visualisation in meditation, all that we are doing is tapping into a resource we already possess naturally, and using to our benefit. You can use a real, concrete object – any stationary object that remains in your field of vision for the duration of the meditation will do. You can also conjure up images in your imagination or even use a combination of both real and imagined images as stimuli. As with meditating on our breathing, the meditation should be relaxed and should not require effort to maintain. Using imagery is similar to having a dream or a daydream but instead of allowing our mind to wander

at random, we are controlling the imagery in a
purposeful manner.

Here is a basic exercise in visualisation:

- As with all other meditations, choose a quiet
  peaceful place where you will not be disturbed.
  Refer to chapter 4 if you need some ideas
- Assume your chosen position and ensure that you
  are comfortable, stable and upright. Although with
  previous meditations, we have kept the eyes shut,
  with this meditation it is necessary to keep the eyes
  open initially.
- Breathe slowly and rhythmically through the
  nostrils and deep into the lungs
- Choose an object within your field of vision that
  will remain there for 15 to 30 minutes or the
  duration of your meditation. One a few minutes
  have elapsed, close your eyes and try to recreate the
  image in your mind's eye. It is unimportant what
  the image is as long as it is pleasant to behold. It
  can be anything, such as a favourite painting or
  ornament, a symbol or even a loved one's face.
  Furthermore, the mental image need not remain the
  same as the concrete one you were just
  contemplating, but can evolve into something quite
  different. As you go further into the meditation, the
  image will become more clear and vivid.
- As with the breathing meditations, your mind will
  tend to wander and your attention will be diverted
  from the image. When this happens, try to remain

patient. Observe the thought that has emerged in your consciousness and gently redirect your attention back to the visual image. Continue to meditate on the image, re-diverting your attention back to the image each time it wanders.

Meditations on Concrete Images

The benefit of using imagery is that combining a thought with an image increases the impact of that thought. The mind's ability to use imagery to promote and strengthen thoughts is widely recognised. For example, language teachers regularly use flashcards when introducing a new word to their students. When learning the vocabulary of a foreign language, it can be difficult to remember the unfamiliar sounds of words and what they mean. But if flashcards are used then the sound becomes linked to a powerful mental image and is therefore easier to retrieve from the memory.

You can choose any object upon which to meditate such as a piece of fruit, a rock, a tree or any inanimate object. I find that a flower is a particularly good object to use when you first begin to meditate using visual images. Not only is it easily obtainable and an aesthetically pleasing subject to behold, but as a living thing, it can be seen to represent your God's or (Gods') creations and the gift of life. It is also particularly suitable for those people who believe in pantheism – the belief that God is identifiable with all things to do with nature.

- As always choose a peaceful place to meditate where you are unlikely to be disturbed.
- Choose a position in which to meditate. For this meditation, sitting on a straight-backed chair in front of a table on which you can place your flower might be the most suitable. For this meditation, it is necessary to keep your eyes open.
- Breathe slowly and rhythmically, filling your lungs with oxygen and feeling your abdomen rise and fall with each breath.
- Empty your mind of all other thoughts and gaze at the flower in front of you. Remain completely relaxed. Try to prevent your gaze from wandering to other objects and attempt to stop any other stray thoughts from entering the mind. You will inevitably be distracted to some degree, particularly with your eyes open, but just remain patient and keep redirecting your gaze and your attention back to the flower.
- Try not to stare too hard or place strain on the eyes and don't be afraid to blink. Just keep on gazing at the flower in a relaxed and passive manner.
- If your eyes start to feel sore, you can close them and try to recreate the image of the flower in your mind's eye. It will be harder to contemplate an imaginary object than it was to contemplate the real thing, but keep the image in your mind and whenever your attention wanders draw it back to the visualised image.
- Once you have been contemplating the image of the

flower for some minutes, you will be aware that your breathing is slow and rhythmical and you will have gone deep into the meditation.

- Continue this exercise for a few minutes and before becoming gradually aware of your surroundings again and ending the meditation.

Meditations on Non-Concrete Images

Visualisation can be used in many ways and it is really up to you to decide what you feel to be most beneficial. As we discovered in the last chapter, many people find that visualising themselves in a situation which they fear can help them to overcome this fear when in the situation for real. In other words, by the power of thought, they re-programme their mind to feel not fear but confidence and self-control.

While visualisation can be used to imagine real-life situations and confront problems in a very literal way, it can also be used symbolically to explore the inner recesses of our minds. This approach is frequently used in psychotherapy as a way of understanding an individual's pattern of behaviour. Often a memory has been deeply buried and can only be accessed by exploring the self-conscious via the imagery that our mind conjures up.

You may feel that you do not possess a particularly powerful imagination but this is probably due to the fact that our natural faculties of fantasy and wonder which we are given free reign when children are suppressed when we become adults. In fact, the more you practise this exercise, the more vivid and powerful your images will become and the more beneficial it will be. The best approach is to take things slowly to begin with without forcing yourself to try and evoke a series of profound images. Just allow the mind to function with no pressure and the meditation will be a productive one.

The best way to approach visualisation, if you do not have a particular purpose in mind is to begin by guiding your thoughts but be open to allowing your subconscious thoughts to rise to the surface. The degree to which you control your thoughts is entirely a personal choice, and it is sometimes best just to see what happens and mould your technique according to how well you feel it is going. While the object of the exercise is to guide the images that come into your mind, do not feel that you have to suppress any that you did not consciously evoke. This would be to ignore the voice of the subconscious and whatever message it may have for us. The aim of meditation using visualisation is not just to replace negative thoughts with more positive ones, but also to explore the unconscious mind to discover the hidden fears and desires which cause these thoughts in the first place.

Before you begin visualisation, it is usually best to have a particular goal in mind, so you know how to direct your thoughts. As you become more advanced, you may find it beneficial to let your mind wander to a greater extent, but for a beginner it is better to keep it more controlled. There are many ways to begin visualisation. Perhaps you have a dilemma that has been troubling you for some time, or you are reaching a crossroads in your life and are unsure of which direction to take. Simply state the problem in your mind and then consider the images that begin to arise in your consciousness. Consider each image in turn and consider why the unconscious evoked these images. Consider what relevance they have to your problem and ask yourself if they provide the key to answering it.

The images that you evoke can be anything - objects, people, places - whatever you feel is more relevant to you. In starting the meditation you may need to work a little bit harder to start things off. As you go further into the meditation, your unconscious mind should start to take over more and more. Acknowledge and consider each image that comes into your mind whether consciously or not. Ask yourself why you might have thought of that particular image and consider what it says about you.

Applying Feng Shui to the Mind

One popular meditation involving the use of visual imagery is to imagine a house in your mind's eye and then apply feng shui to the interior of this house.

Feng shui literally translated from the Chinese means Wind and Water, and it is a system that the Chinese use to design buildings which takes into account the positive and negative influences of our surroundings. The Chinese believe that by placing certain objects in certain positions, they can have a positive or negative effect on their future financial prospects, health and love life. If you wish to know more about Feng Shui, there is a book in the same series as this one.

- As before, choose quiet, tranquil place in which you can meditate successfully.
- Get into a position of your choice. Ensure that you are comfortable, stable and the spine is straight, the face pointing straight-ahead. With this meditation, it is appropriate to keep the eyes shut.
- Take deep, slow regular breaths
- In your mind, picture a house that you feel accurate reflects your personality. This can be similar to the house you live in, or it can be entirely of your imagination. Try and make the image of the house as vivid and realistic as possible.
- Now imagine entering each room of the hose, one by one. For each room you can choose an area of your life that you wish it to represent. For example, one room can reflect your love life, another can reflect your spiritual side – you can choose whatever you feel has most relevance to you.
- When you enter a room, concentrate on how it makes you feel. Is there anything that you would like to change? Anything that makes you feel uncomfortable? Enter each room, one by one, and ask yourself the same questions.

- As with any meditation, your mind will wander, and your attention will be diverted from your feng shui house. Again, when this happen, it is important to remain patient. Acknowledge these stray thoughts as they enter your head. It could be they are of relevance to the meditation this time. Then re-direct your attention back to the room you are in.

This meditation is more complex than others we have tried, and it may take a few attempts before you feel the benefits from it but bear with it as it will become more productive each time you try it. It is a good way of exploring your feelings towards each area of your live and of highlighting the parts which you would like to change – parts that otherwise may have remained buried in the unconscious.

For more visual imagery meditation, and for other ideas for meditations in general, see chapter 12.

CHAPTER 11
Insight Meditations

In Buddhism, there are said to be three universal characteristics of existence. These are the idea that existence is impermanent, the idea that there is nothing that can provide us with lasting satisfaction, and the idea that nothing is fixed or permanent including our own identities. Buddhists believe that these are more than theories and that they actually reflect the reality of existence. Although these universal characteristics of existence may seem unlikely to many, Buddhists would argue that this is because we live in a spiritually impoverished and consumer driven society where objects are continually sold to us as being a major source of satisfaction. In order to overcome the illusory ideas that they may have absorbed from their surroundings and familiarise themselves with the true nature of existence, Buddhists perform insight meditation or vipassana meditation on these characteristics and on related themes.

Insight Meditation is employed by Buddhists in an attempt to contemplate the true nature of existence, as this is a necessary stage in achieving enlightenment.

With practise, insight meditations are said to become effortless and you should eventually be able to gain an intuitive insight into the nature of reality without having to exert much thought. However, as these are difficult concepts for the novice to grasp, it is easier to begin meditating on various aspects of these three universal characteristics of existence. Perhaps when you have mastered these meditations and grasped the concept behind them, you will begin to intuitively perceive this Buddhist notion of reality. In this chapter, I have included meditations on subjects considered to be important to the Buddhist faith that all relate to these three characteristics of existence and are all regularly practised by Buddhists. The meditations are a meditation on appreciating life, a meditation on love and compassion, a meditation on impermanence, a meditation on mortality and a meditation on suffering.

While these meditations are Buddhist in origin, they are not of a specifically devotional nature, and can therefore be practised by people of any religion. You can select one that you feel is most suitable or even use these as inspiration for making up your own meditations on other aspects of existence that you feel are relevant to you.

Meditation on Appreciating Life

For everything that lives is holy, life delights in life.
William Blake; *America: A Prophecy*

Buddhists believe that meditating on appreciating life allows us to put our problems into perspective and to appreciate just how much potential we possess as human beings. The extent to which we enjoy our lives is said to be determined not only by extraneous factors that we cannot control, but also by our own perceptions of the world and the decisions we make as a result of these perceptions.

Most of us are guilty of failing to appreciate life. We tend to focus on the negative aspects and when things go wrong, we fail to take much responsibility for this. We have a tendency to blame other extraneous factors and often do not even admit to ourselves that we may have had a part in causing our own bad luck. Buddhists would claim that this is down to the fact that our behaviour is governed by a series of fallacious perceptions of our external surroundings as well as by our unconscious drives and desires of which we are usually unaware. Therefore, we cannot really help making wrong decisions sometimes, as we can only use the information that we have.

It is a Buddhist belief that we have to explore the misperceptions and unconscious drives that we may have or we will never find a solution to our problems and will continue to display dysfunctional behaviour. Through meditation, we can explore our perceptions of the world and our own unconscious urges that govern our behaviour. In doing this, we can change those patterns of thought that have led us to make the wrong decision in the past, or to cause unhappiness to others.

Buddhists believe that most of our problems spring from our attitudes to life and our low self-image. It is generally accepted as a truism that most humans only appreciate life when it is threatened in some way or changed for the worse. After a loss of any kind, it is common to hear people lament that they never fully appreciated what they had until it was gone, This is something that most of us are guilty of. Consider this quote from Shakespeare's *Hamlet*:

> What a piece of work is man! How noble in reason!
> How infinite in faculties!
> In form and moving, how express and admirable!
> In action, how like an angel!
> In apprehension, how like a god! The beauty of the
> world! The paragon of animals!
> And yet to me, what is this quintessence of dust?
>
> *(Act II, scene II)*

The tendency of humans to become weighed down by their own problems is timeless. In this quotation, Hamlet is aware of the potential of human existence, but has been so overcome by depression and so absorbed in his own problems that he can no longer appreciate or even believe in the finer qualities of human beings. Human beings have huge potential, but because of many factors, including the stressful nature of modern life and the sometimes unrewarding careers we may have fallen into, we forget about this potential and instead focus on our flaws and limitations. We exacerbate these limitations whilst diminishing our achievements, and are far more likely to confirm those negative perceptions of our character on little evidence than we are to refute or challenge them.

Buddhists believe that it is possible for us to become more happy and contented individuals whatever the circumstances of our individual lives are, but first we must become more familiar with our own thought processes so that we can then modify our behaviour. This can be a lengthy task and one that will not be achieved instantly. It also requires us to be honest and accepting of our limitations and faults as well as our good qualities. We cannot take steps to improve our characters until we face up to what our faults actually are. This meditation is very similar to the meditations on negative thought patterns that we explored in chapter 9, but it is designed to examine our whole character and perceptions of the world, rather than just targeting one particular negative aspect we are already aware of.

When we come to examine our problems more closely, most of them will probably seem quite minor and surmountable. Human beings have a tendency to allow themselves to be overwhelmed by quite trivial worries. It is our distorted perception of our problems and worries that causes them to become blown out of proportion. We become too close to a problem to analyse it objectively and fail to see that most of the time it is something that can be overcome with effort and self-analysis.

While this is a meditation on a Buddhist philosophy, meditating on appreciation for live is suitable for anyone who wishes to obtain a more positive outlook on life and is said to be particularly beneficial for those people who suffer from depression. It is believed to help us to target negative feeling such as depression in a logical manner, replacing unnecessarily defeatist attitudes with more accurate, positive ones. Once we are reminded of our own potential, and the degree to which we have control of our lives, we should gradually start to develop a more positive and optimistic outlook. This increases our enthusiasm for life which, in turn, increases the effort that we put into our lives and also makes us more resilient when things go wrong. Furthermore, once we have recognised that our situation is not as bad as we had feared, we can become less absorbed in our own problems and more compassionate to the sufferings of others in the world.

THE MEDITATION

- As the meditations we have looked at so far have been fairly structured and basic, you may find that this one feels a little strange at first. As usual, find a suitable quiet and peaceful place to meditate. Select a comfortable position and make sure that the posture is straight and the head facing directly in front of you.
- If you wish to warm up and ensure that your mind is alert and focused, you could try one of the

breathing meditations that we looked at in chapter 7 for a few minutes.

- When you are ready to begin, start to consider your attitude to life. Consider if you have any negative feelings about any part of your life, and if there are any factors about yourself and your character that you would like to change. If there is nothing in particular bothering you at the moment then think back to a time when you had a problem that seemed insurmountable at the time. Try to pinpoint why you felt like that. Think about whether or not this was a rational response to the situation and if there is anything else that you could have done to improve the situation.

Meditating on feelings on hopelessness and despair should allow you to work out what it was that triggered them in the first place. It should also allow you to place them into perspective and prevent them from worrying you in the future, leaving you free to enjoy and appreciate life. If you are finding it hard to lose those feelings of hopelessness and despair, then you might find it helpful to remember situations you have been in that were worse than your current situation, or even imagine other situations you could be in which are much worse than your own.

Meditation on Love and Compassion

> Compassion and love are not mere luxuries. As the
> source of both internal and external peace, they are
> fundamental to the continued survival of our
> species.
>
> The Dalai Lama in *The Times*, June 1999

Buddhists believe that meditating on love and
compassion will enhance our ability to feel love and
compassion towards other people as well as towards
ourselves. This is also said to make us more tolerant of
our own minor worries and more considerate towards
others.

We are all capable of experiencing the emotions of
love and compassion, and although this capacity is
boundless, most of us do fail to use it most of the time
and tend to save these finer feelings for our close
family and friends. However, Buddhists believe that
this meditation can teach us to extend these feelings to
everyone in the world thus making us kinder, more
understanding people and improving our relationships
with others. This can be a very difficult concept to
grasp at first. In our society, we are encouraged to
foster a 'survival of the fittest' philosophy, which means
that we tend to look out for our own, and our own
family's welfare, whilst ignoring the plight of others.
Meditating on love and compassion is thought to
render us more calm and carefree people, as well as
making us more approachable to other people.

Beginners are said to find this meditation difficult. It is hard to feel love and compassion to those people that we are currently feel neutral towards, never mind those people that we actually feel animosity towards. The goal of this meditation is to feel love and compassion towards everyone, no matter what their faults are. This includes minor acquaintances, people we dislike and even those people who have wronged us in some way.

This meditation should help us to overcome the judgements that we make on other people. Buddhists believe that we have a limitless quantity of love to share and this meditation allows us to use this. If we practise this meditation regularly then we should find that our previous feelings of hostility towards those people we do not like will turn to feelings of compassion and love.

THE MEDITATION
- As with our other meditations, find a quiet, tranquil place in which to meditate. Select a suitable position, as always making sure that the posture is straight and the head facing directly in front of you.
- If you feel the need to warm up, remember you can try one of the breathing meditations that we looked at in chapter 7 for a few minutes.
- Begin by bringing to mind all of the people in your life at the moment. Start with your immediate family and close friends. Now move onto those who you feel animosity towards and those who may

have hurt and betrayed you. Now try to think of all of the people in the universe. You can visualise them if this helps you. Try to remain relaxed even though you may be thinking of people that you do not usually feel comfortable around.

- Try to feel a sense of empathy with all of these people. Imagine some of the things that they could have in common with you. Imagine being able to feel love towards all of these people, including the ones you feel angry towards and the ones you do not even know. Try to remember that no one is perfect, and you should not let yourself be overly critical of other people's faults.

- Now focus on the feeling of loving someone. Keep your mind focussed on this emotion and allow it to pervade your body and mind.

- In order to experience true feelings of compassion towards others, it is important that you first feel this emotion towards yourself. We are often hard on ourselves, and while it is important that we are aware of our faults, it is equally important that we are compassionate towards ourselves. Try to direct this feeling of love and compassion that you have been meditating on towards yourself.

- Now let this feeling of love to flow out towards the other people that you have been thinking of. Begin with those who are closest to you – your partner, family and close friends. This should be an easy thing to do.

- Keep a hold these feelings of love and compassion

and, this time, direct them towards those who you feel a sense of animosity towards, those who you feel perhaps have wronged you in some way in the past. You should try to feel genuine love and compassion towards them. Allow your positive feelings to flow out towards them, replacing any trace of negative emotion you may have towards them. This may seem unnatural at first, as it goes against the behavioural patterns that most people usually follow, but is said to become easier with practice.

- Now, project these emotions of love and compassion that you have been meditating upon out towards all of those people that you are merely acquainted with. Your entire being should now be filled with feelings of love and compassion.
- Concentrate on this feeling for a little longer. Now let it flow out to everyone in the universe particularly those who may be vulnerable or in danger and who need it the most.

Buddhists believe that everyone deserves our love and compassion, not just our family and friends. You should try to hold on to this feeling of love that you have just been generating and use it in your daily life. It is often our own negative emotions that prevent us from feeling love and compassion towards others, so you should continue to work on these feelings and they will become more readily invoked and will feel more natural.

Meditation on Impermanence

> Everything is ephemeral: both that which
> remembers and that which is remembered.
>
> Marcus Aurelius; *Meditations*

Meditating on impermanence, one of the universal characteristics of existence, is said by Buddhists to increase our sense of resilience and make us more accepting of change. It is also said to allow us to appreciate our lives more and make more out of them.

It is a scientific fact that the universe is in a constant state of flux and things are changing and evolving all the time. Some changes are a part of our everyday lives such as growing older, forming new relationships and changing jobs. Other changes such as evolution take place at a slower rate and do not tend to impinge on our lives too much.

While Buddhists are accepting of the fact that constant change is a fact of existence, this can be a difficult concept for many other people to grasp. We spend a fortune on face creams and modify our diets in an attempt to stop the onslaught of age. We are creatures of habit and find it difficult to accept change even when it is of a positive nature. We have a tendency to cling on to our ideas and opinions, often ignoring any argument that contradicts them. Unlike Buddhists who do not believe that the individual is an eternal, fixed entity, we view our own personalities as though they were permanent and unchanging. We believe that we are certain types of people rather than just considering our behaviour according to each situation we find ourselves in.

By meditating on impermanence, it is said that we will come to accept that the world is in a constant state of change. Buddhists believe that it is important to be aware of this as it means that we are more accepting of change and we will not resist change when it is of a positive nature. It also allows us to accept the random events that life tends to throw at us with a more calm and resilient manner. Rather than constantly asking why these things have to happen to us, we will calmly accept that change affects everyone and move on to making the best out of the situation. Meditating on the impermanence and transience of all that surrounds us is also a useful preparation for the meditation on mortality which we will go on to look at in the next chapter.

THE MEDITATION
- As always, find a suitable place and position to meditate in. If you like, you can focus your concentration in preparation for this meditation by counting your breaths or doing one of the other meditations.
- Focus you attention on your own body. Visualise your body and all the activity that is constantly going on inside it - the oxygen flows in and out, the blood pumps around the body, and the cells constantly reproduce and then die.

- Now visualise yourself as a child and think of how you have aged since then. Think of the dreams and ambitions that you once fostered and of how different they are to your goals in life now.
- Now think of people who were once a part of your life, perhaps even close friends, that you are not even in touch with now. Meditate on how your circumstances have changed throughout your life.
- Continue this meditation for a few minutes. Once you feel as though you have thoroughly grasped the transitory nature of things you can finish the meditation.

Remember the Buddhist believe that everything is constantly changing including our ideas, our surroundings, and ourselves. The next time when your life changes in some way, perhaps you should try not to dwell on the loss you may be feeling but instead look to the future. In Buddhism, it is said that it is only when you accept that everything is in a continual state of flux, that you will truly understand the conditions in which we live and you can begin to truly enjoy life.

Meditation on Mortality

La Mort ne suprend point le sage; il est toujours pret a partir.
(Death does not take the wise man by surprise; he is always prepared to leave.)

Jean de la Fontaigne; *Le Mourir et Mort*

Buddhists believe that meditating on mortality is said to increase our appreciation of live and to stop us from clinging onto possessions and relationships to an unhealthy degree. It is also said to prepare us for death so that we might die with a positive, calm frame of mind ready for our next incarnation.

Many people feel uncomfortable when they first come to meditate on death as it is seen as a morbid subject. People view death as a negative experience and believe that we should only meditate on positive thoughts. We are reluctant to leave our loved ones behind, we are afraid that death will be a painful, frightening experience and we have a deep-seated belief that our sense of self is real and somehow eternal. Death is also perceived by many of us as being a journey into the unknown and this fills us with fear, worry and other negative emotions. However, according to Buddhist philosophy, this fear of death and unwillingness to face up to its approach only intensifies the discomfort we feel regarding the subject. It is important that we realise that death is an inevitable part of life and not something to be feared but accepted.

While Buddhists are accepting of the fact that our sense of ourselves is not a permanent entity, it is natural for us to find it hard to accept that, at some point in the future, we shall no longer exist and the world will carry on anyway. The human instinct for survival is a powerful force and, if faced with the choice, most of us would choose a life of unhappiness over no life at all. However, Buddhists believe that we have to accept that the day will come when we will die and put this into perspective so that when the day comes we will be prepared. The biggest difficulty is separating our egotistical notion of our own character and the experience of life itself, as we have never known the two as separate entities.

Buddhists feel that it is necessary that we understand that nothing is permanent. Everything around us is in a constant state of flux. We do not exist as permanent, unwavering entities. The sooner we appreciate the transience of life we can put the event of our own death into perspective and appreciate it as a consequence of life and an inevitable conclusion to our existence.

Meditating on mortality is highly beneficial both for Buddhists and non-Buddhists alike, as it allows us to fully appreciate our existence and encourages us to make the most out of the life we have been given. We have been given the opportunity to lead useful valuable, worthwhile lives. We each have been imbued with the potential to increase our knowledge, to broaden our minds, to exert love and compassion to other humans and to ourselves, and to reach our full potential as human beings. Death is inevitable and can come at any time. If we remain constantly aware of this fact of life, we will always strive to achieve the most out of life that we possibly can and not to waste time on unimportant activities or on feeling negative emotions towards others or ourselves.

Buddhists regard death as an inevitable and useful fact of life. They believe that remaining aware of the fact that they are going to die allows them to realise the importance of making the most of the here and now whilst preventing them from dwelling on the past or worrying about what the future may bring. This in turn is said to leave them more content and realistic and more able to put problems into perspective. This meditation is referred to as the Nine-Point meditation on Death and it comes from the Lam Rim Tibetan Buddhist tradition.

THE MEDITATION

- As usual, find an appropriate place to meditate and get into a comfortable position of relaxed consciousness, making sure the posture remains upright. As always, you can prepare yourself for this meditation, by practising one of the breathing meditations we focused on in an earlier chapter.
- Once your body is relaxed and your mind ready to focus on the subject of our meditation, you can begin.
- he first three points in the nine-point meditation on death all explore the idea that death is inevitable. In order to meditate on this idea, first consider the idea that death comes to us all, no matter who we are. It does not matter what your position in life is, as you will eventually die just like everyone else. Buddhists believe that you cannot escape the fact even if you are rich, famous, successful or powerful,

as when we die, everyone becomes equal.

- Think of all the people that know, from your close friends and family to your acquaintances. Contemplate the fact that, one day, these people will all die. Contemplate this fact for a few minutes until you feel that you have grasped it fully.

- Now, contemplate the fact that even as you sit reading this book, your life is running out. No matter how technologically advanced the world becomes, it is impossible to stop the progression of time. It is easy to forget that as we go about our daily lives, our lives are becoming shorter all the time.

- Now you have grasped the concept that death is inevitable and coming closer all the time, think of how you spend your time in life. Estimate the amount of time that you spend on tasks which can be described as useful, such as reading a mind-expanding book, showing love and compassion to those around you, or developing a more tolerant and broad-minded attitude. Now estimate how much time you spent on less useful tasks such as watching poor quality television, gossiping about people in an uncharitable way and making judgements on others. If you have been wasting your time on non-profitable activities, you can end this and decide to start spending more time on more useful, life-enriching activities.

- The next three points in the nine-point meditation on death all explore the fact that the time of death is usually unknown. To meditate on this idea, focus your attention on the knowledge that each of our lives is of an uncertain duration. We know approximately how long a human life lasts but this can vary. Life can also be cut short prematurely by many causes and at any time. We can look after our health in order to try to help prolong life but ultimately it is out of our control.

- Now contemplate the fact that you could die at any time of a completely unexpected cause. Think of all the hundreds of ways that people can die and of all of the unexpected accidents that are reported in the newspapers every day. Contemplate the complete uncertainty as to how long your life will last and imagine how you would feel if it were to be cut short today. Consider if you would have any regrets, or if there is something that you have been putting off until the future that you would wish that you had done. When you feel that you have managed to comprehend the fact that death can come to any of us at any time, meditate on it for a few minutes.
- Now focus your mind on the human body and how vulnerable and easily damaged it can be. While the human body is a source of constant wonder in its ability to heal itself and reproduce, you should remember that it is also very vulnerable. Think of the numerous illnesses there are that can damage the body and sometimes prove fatal. Meditate on this thought for a few minutes.
- The final three points in this meditation all explore

the idea that only spiritual insight will be of any use to us when we die. In order to meditate on this point, turn your thoughts to imagining what it would be like to be dying. Imagine how little comfort there would be in the things that you normally enjoy, such as food, alcohol, music, and literature. Contemplate your possessions and career and then consider how little use they are to you now. Think of all the loved ones you have in your life and contemplate the fact that when you die you may never see them again. Buddhists consider this part of the inevitable experience of death. This is said to help them prepare both for the grief of losing loved ones as well as preparing them for when they themselves die and leave loved ones behind.

• Like people of many other religions, Buddhists believe that we will not be able to take material possessions, money, power and status with us when we die. As material possessions play such an important role in our lives, it is hard for us to accept that they will become irrelevant when we die. Buddhists believe that the only thing we can be sure that has any lasting value in our lives is the wisdom we have acquired and passed onto others, and the compassion we have displayed to others. Fully accepting this premise is said to have a positive influence on how we spend our lives.

A summary of the Nine-Point Meditation on Death:

A. Death is inevitable for everyone:
  1. Everyone must die.
  2. Our lives are decreasing every second.
  3. We only devote a small amount of time to increasing our spiritual insight or dharma.

B. The time of death is unknown:
  1. The duration of life is unknown.
  2. Many things can cause death.
  3. The human body is fragile.

C. Only spiritual insight can help us at the point of death:
  1. Possessions will not be able to help us.
  2. Family and friends will not be able to help us.
  3. Our body will not be able to help us.

Meditating on death can be a difficult and often emotionally draining thing to do, particularly when you first begin to try it, and it can take a great deal of practise to fully grasp the concepts of this meditation. However, Buddhists believe that it is only when you come to fully comprehended the inevitability of death can you begin to achieve your fullest potential in life.

Meditation on Suffering

> A man who fears suffering, is already suffering from
> what he fears.
>
> Michel de Montaigne; *Essais* 1580

Meditating on suffering is believed by Buddhists to allow us to maintain a realistic view of life. It is also said to increase our feelings of love and compassion towards those who are less well off than us and allow us to be critical with a view to improving our own lives.

It is easy to become despondent when we look at the world and see constant violence and even people with a strong religious faith find it hard to comprehend why there is so much starvation, violence and cruelty in the world.

As with meditating on death, many beginners find this meditation difficult at first. There is so much suffering around us that it can seem easier to try to shut it out instead of deliberately drawing our attention towards it. Buddhists believe that the Western view of life tends to be unrealistic as we expect to be happy and comfortable, as though it was a basic right. When things go wrong, as they often do, we are prone to feeling anger and even indignation. It is a tenet of Buddhism that we should realise that suffering is an inevitable part of existence. In fact, suffering is often considered to be necessary to make us see that part of our life is not going well and we may need to change our behaviour in some way in order to amend this.

Meditating on the extent of suffering both in our lives and in those around us, is the first step we can take towards alleviating this suffering. If we change our expectation of life and accept that suffering is as much a part of life as pleasure and has to be tolerated to some degree, then it will make us more stoical towards suffering. This will also make us more appreciative of those times when things are going well.

The main objective of this meditation on suffering however is to pinpoint the source of suffering in our own lives, so we can try to be rid of it. It is a Buddhist belief that most of the unhappiness and discontent we suffer from are due to unrealistic expectations from the world, so if we could only change our expectations, we could put an end to or at least diminish our suffering. For example, when we meditate on the Buddhist universal characteristics of the universe and come to accept the limited duration of our lives and the ultimate unimportance of material possessions and of relationships with others, we should become more at peace with ourselves, and the world.

Accepting these universal characteristics is a very difficult goal to achieve, though. We are socially conditioned from birth to acquire material possessions, to strive for happiness, to devote time and energy to our relationships with others. It can be very difficult for us to come to terms with the fact that none of these things are really that important, and to place all our hopes and expectation on them is only going to lead to more suffering and disappointment.

THE MEDITATION

- Once more, select an appropriate place in which to meditate, then assume the position that you are going to meditate in.
- It can be useful to begin a meditation on suffering by thinking of times that you have suffered in your own life. Try thinking of times when you have suffered from minor illnesses, such as a headache or a cold. Try to recreate in your mind the discomfort you experienced and remain focused on that feeling of suffering.
- Now turn your mind to a time when you perhaps suffered from a more serious illness. This time recreate in your mind not only the discomfort that you felt but also the emotional distress that this brought with it. Try to remember what this felt like and hold the feeling in your mind for a few minutes.
- Once you have contemplated this physical suffering for a few minutes, turn your attention to remembering occasions when you have suffered emotionally. Think of times when you have tortured yourself with negative emotions such as anger, jealousy or fear. These are human emotions that we all suffer from but Buddhists believe that moderation should be practised at all times so it is important to try and overcome them.
- Try examining your current state of mind. Consider

if you are suffering any negative emotions at the moment and imagine how you will suffer from events in the future such as a loved one dying. Hold that feeling and contemplate it for a few moments.

- Now look beyond you own suffering and try to experience the suffering of others. Begin by imagining those close to you such as your partner, your family and your close friends. Imagine what problems they may have and what it must be like to experience and feel empathy for the way they are suffering.

- Now expand this feeling of empathy towards everyone in the world including people you may feel hostility towards as well as those you have never even met. Consider what kind of suffering is going on and empathise with what these people are feeling.

Buddhists believe that practising this meditation will make you gradually amend your expectations to become more realistic, thus making you a more calm and stable person. It will also allow you to feel more compassion towards other people.

CHAPTER 12
Ten More Exercises in Meditation

Here are some more exercises that you can try when meditating. Choose any one of these or use them as inspiration to make up your own. As with any meditation, it is a good idea to practise a breathing meditation before any of these exercises, to prepare your mind and body for what is to come.

1 Working Meditation

This meditation is said to be useful for those people whose lives are so hectic that they cannot fit in a regular time to meditate. It is a way of meditating whilst performing an activity or chore at the same time. It is very flexible compared to more traditional methods of meditation, can be easily slotted into your daily routine and, furthermore, is simple to learn. It is designed to increase your enjoyment of and improve your performance at whichever activity you choose to focus on whilst doing this meditation.

When you are choosing the activity you wish to focus on during the working meditation, there are several factors to take into account. If you are to make this meditation a regular part of your routine, then it could be argued that it is probably best to choose an activity that you enjoy doing. However, it can also be argued that if you have a busy schedule, then you can choose an activity that you would have to be doing anyway, but consider to be a waste of time. Examples of suitable activities can be washing the dishes, vacuuming, cleaning the bathroom or washing the car. Also, it is probably best to choose something that takes about the same length of time as a standard meditation, which is usually about 15 to 30 minutes in length. Try not to choose a task that will take much longer than this as this could prove to be physically and mentally draining and this will only affect the quality of the meditation. It is also best to choose something that you can perform on your own, so that you are not reliant on other people to be able to do it.

When practising this meditation, it is important that you maintain a positive attitude towards the job at hand. Try to enjoy each part of the task that you are performing and focus your awareness upon each part of the task. Incorporate parts of other meditations that you have performed into this one. For example, remember to breathe correctly so that you feel your abdomen raise and lower as you inhale and exhale. As with other meditations, do not let your mind wander whilst you are performing your task. If you feel that you have let your attention slip, gently redirect it back towards the task you are performing. Do not allow yourself to become tense and if you are feeling tired then take a break for a minute or two until this feeling has passed. Do not concern yourself with thoughts of having to finish for a certain time and do not rush the task at hand.

You will find that by focusing your awareness on the task in this way and carrying out a meditation whilst performing this task will make that task far more enjoyable and rewarding. You will feel rejuvenated both during and afterwards and the task will no longer be something that you look upon with dread. The quality of your work should also be seen to improve.

2   Journey Meditation

This is a popular form of meditation that uses a combination of imaginative powers and visual imagery, the form of meditation that we looked at in chapter 10. This meditation is particularly good for those people with a strong visual imagination who find it particularly relaxing to be in tranquil surroundings. It is like taking a holiday without having to leave your own front room and you are left with no expenses or suitcases full of dirty laundry at the end of it. This is said to be an especially good meditation to do if you are feeling lethargic or run down, as it has a highly invigorating effect.

In order to practise this meditation, first it is necessary to assume a comfortable position. By this time, you should have a fairly good idea of which positions work best for you.

Breathe in slowly and deeply for a few minutes and feel the stress leave your body, as your breathing becomes light, regular and effortless.

Now conjure up in your mind's eye a place where you feel that you could meditate in peace and tranquillity. This can be anywhere you like. It can be a place abroad that you have visited before or a place that you would like to go. It can be a real place or it can be entirely a work of your imagination. It can be far away, or it can be in the town where you live. As long as imagining yourself in this place makes you feel safe and calm then it is suitable for incorporation into the journey meditation.

A popular destination for the journey meditation is imagining that you are on a beach. This is probably due to the fact that people associate beaches with holidays, which are a time for relaxation, away from all the stresses and strains of everyday life. Other ideas for destinations for the journey meditation are to imagine that you are in the countryside, in a park, or in a forest.

Whatever destination you have chosen, picture yourself there now. Start to build a set if you like in your mind's eye. If you have chosen a beach for your destination, then imagine the sound of the waves lapping up to the shore. Feel the warmth of the sun envelope your skin. Picture the clear blue sky and the golden sand. Are there any flora or fauna in your ideal destination? Are there other people on the beach? Or perhaps you have chosen to go to a secluded island where you are unlikely to be disturbed.

Listen to the sounds of seagulls in the distance, or the rustling of trees in the breeze. Try to imagine your destination as vividly as though you were really there. Do not worry if your mind wanders – simply draw it back to visualising your destination. Do this for approximately 20 minutes and then gradually become aware of your external surroundings and end the meditation. This meditation can be so enjoyable that you may find that you are particularly reluctant to end it.

3   Movement Meditation

Movement meditation is very similar to the discipline of yoga. This meditation uses a combination of breathing and gentle movements. It is particularly useful for those who find more visual meditations difficult or for those who like to feel that they are doing gentle exercise whilst meditating. During movement meditation, the individual is said to draw energy from the earth – energy that is regarded as being the source of all life on earth. This is a good meditation to practice first thing in the morning as the gentle movements that it incorporates warm the body up for the rest of the day, whilst the meditation itself leaves the mind refreshed and alert.

To practice this meditation, first of make sure you

are breathing correctly – the abdomen should move up and down as you inhale and exhale, and the breaths themselves should not be too shallow. An appropriate position for the movement meditation is to squat on the floor. Your feet should be apart, your legs slightly bent, your muscles relaxed, and your hips and pelvis should stay loose. Feel the gravity pulling you down into the Earth and maintain a sense of balance by imagining that the soles of your feet have taken root in the soil. Imagine the centre of the Earth to contain a visible energy – the source of all life. You can visualise this in any way that you find to be helpful. Many people imagine this as a ball of light that emanates warmth and energy. Feel yourself connecting to this and imagine waves of this energy flowing up through your feet and all the way through to the top of your body.

Now that you are imbued with energy, you can start to move. You can choose any movements that you feel comfortable with and if you are short of ideas then it is sometimes useful to look to nature for inspiration. For example, imagine that you begin as being a closed bud on a plant. Now continuing to imagine yourself as this bud, pretend that you are beginning to bloom and develop into a flower. Gradually straighten your spine and stretch your body up and out towards the sun. Uncurl your limbs and stretch them out as far as possible, emulating the movements of a flower in bloom. Other ideas for movements are to emulate the undulations of a snake or to gently sway side to side like a tree in a breeze. You can also walk about or even dance if you like. This meditation is also suitable for performing to music to help create the right mood and to give you some kind of rhythm to follow.

All this time, your attention should stay focussed on the movements of your body. Allow yourself to become lost in the feeling of this movement and feel your limbs and trunk become more relaxed and flexible the longer that you perform this meditation. Feel this flexibility spread throughout your body, especially towards those areas that have built-up tension. Continue this for around 20 minutes then gradually direct your awareness back to your external surroundings.

4 Body Scan Meditation

This meditation combines a visual, imaginative approach to meditation whilst remaining aware of your own body. This meditation depends upon the power of thought and visualisation and is useful if there are any parts of your body that are giving you pain or discomfort. This is very similar to the relaxation exercise that we looked at in chapter 8, but this time you are not moving each part of your body, or systematically relaxing each part – you are simply being aware of them and visualising them in your mind's eye.

To practise this meditation, it is recommended that you lie flat on your back against the floor. Feel free to use a rug or mat if you find this uncomfortable at all. This position allows you to visualise your body more effectively whilst provide a stable base on which to meditate. You legs should remain uncrossed, your arms should lie by your sides with your palms facing upwards towards the ceiling. You can have your eyes open or closed but it is probably easier if you keep them closed as you are going to scan your entire body, not with your eyes but with your imagination.

Now focus on your breathing for a few minutes, in order to prepare yourself for the meditation. Once you begin to feel comfortable, relaxed and mentally alert, you can begin the body scan.

First of all, direct your attention towards the toes on your right foot. Do not look at them directly but visualise them in your mind's eye and feel the sensation of them. One way of keeping your attention focused on your toes is to imagine the blood flowing through the body and carrying oxygen to the part that you are currently focussing on. Keep you attention on your toes and if you mind wanders simply redirect it back to your toes. Focus on the toes for a few minutes and once you have done this, move your attention to the toes on your left foot and use the same procedure for them.

Continue this practise, using all parts of the lower body to visualise and focus your attention on. Work up from the toes, to each entire foot, to the calves, to the thighs, then the buttocks and stomach. Then do the same thing for the upper body, moving from the chest, to the inner organs, to the arms and the shoulders. Pay particular attention to any areas that give you problems – such as the ovaries if you suffer from period pains or endometriosis, the lungs if you suffer from asthma, or the back if you suffer from back pain. Visualise these areas as being whole and well again, and witness the pain leaving them. Often just visualising something is a powerful enough tool to make it happen.

Now continue the same practice, this time using the head as your focus. Move your focus towards each particular part, visualising them as you go. Start with the jaw then move to the mouth, the lips, the nose, the eyes and the forehead. Then move your attention to the hair and then finally direct your attention away from yourself and towards an awareness of the entire universe and your place in it.

5   Healing Meditation

In the Body Scan mediation, we considered the possibility of making problem areas of our body better just by looking at them. In chapter 9, we explored the power of thought and visualisation in changing your life. We will now explore these ideas further with the Healing Meditation. The power of the mind when healing the body is a wondrous thing and a recognised medical phenomenon known as the placebo effect. The placebo effect is when we believe we are being cured and this belief itself is enough to cure us. Studies have been done to show that patients can be given pills made entirely of sugar and told that this is medicine, and the belief that they are being treated for their illness is enough to make them feel better.

Our bodies are capable of all sorts of miraculous feats and the mind usually has some part to play in this. For example, we have all heard the story of a mother being able to lift a car by herself because her child's life depended upon it. Something she would never have been able to do under normal circumstances. This was due to the mind giving off a signal to the body that extra strength was needed and the body complied despite this task being beyond its normal limits. Our body is also capable of repairing itself when damaged and is constantly regenerating cells and renewing old tissue. This natural ability to heal combined with the power of the mind is what makes the healing meditation effective. There is no guarantee that this meditation will cure disease but the power of the mind to heal the body is a long recognised phenomenon and is at least worth a try.

As with any meditation, choose a comfortable position and prepare to meditate. Take deep breaths and feel the tension begin to leave your body. You can now begin.

In your mind's eye, start by visualising areas in your body that have been damaged in some way. You may have cut yourself, for example. Visualise the damaged cells that surround the cut. Watch them gradually begin to regenerate and heal themselves. Now imagine all the injured or damaged cells in your body and do the same. Visualise your body as being whole and free from injury of any kind.

Now move your focus to the immune system. When the body is damaged in some way, the immune system is put into action and cells are released that kills the unhealthy cells that are damaging the body. Visualise these cells. Imagine that they are multiplying and killing off any cells that are threatening to make you unwell.

Imagine that your body becomes filled with the energy to heal itself. Visualise this energy as it imbues your entire body and then spreads to every area, focusing around those areas that may have suffered from damage of some kind. Watch as each part of your body becomes healed and purified. Now watch this healing energy leave your body, leaving everything regenerated and healed.

If you are currently suffering pain or discomfort in any area of your body, or if you have problems that centre around any area in your body then try this. Visualise the area that is causing you pain. See it as being composed of millions of tiny little cells. Now visualise the nerves in this part of the body that are sending signals of this pain to receptors in your brain. Now imagine a healing energy enter your body and head straight for this area. Watch as the damaged cells repair themselves. Once they are healed, visualise the nerves become soothed. The signals of pain should now cease. Your body should now be filled with a sense of relief that the pain has now gone.

This meditation is most effective if you are convinced of its power to heal. Any scepticism can prevent any beneficial effects. It is widely recognised throughout the medical community that the belief that the body will heal and a positive attitude can promote healing, whether this be to cure a common cold or to fight against a life-threatening illness like cancer.

6   *Forgiveness Meditation*

We often make life more difficult for ourselves by carrying around feelings of bitterness and resentment towards others and refusing to let go of grudges. This meditation is the perfect antidote for these negative behavioural patterns and allows us to feel a sense of forgiveness towards those who may have wronged us in the past. This is similar to the meditation on love in chapter 11, but provides a more specific focus.

Choose a suitable environment and position in which to meditate. Start to take deep, slow breaths. Focus on your breathing for a few minutes until you become relaxed and alert. Now each time you inhale, imagine that your entire body is being infused with a sense of forgiveness and that each time you exhale, you release all those pent up feelings of anger and resentment towards others or even towards yourself. When you inhale, hold your breaths for a few moments in order to allow this forgiveness more time to spread throughout your body. Imagine forgiveness as a blue light and resentment as a red light. Now imagine the red light start to disappear as the blue light fills your entire body from head to toe and your body gradually becomes purified and filled with the power of forgiveness.

Once you have meditated on this feeling of forgiveness for a few minutes, it is time to turn your attention towards someone you feel that you need to forgive. This can be anyone – someone who has wronged you in the past, someone who has offended you in some way, or even just someone who has caused you irritation in a minor way. Harness all that forgiveness that has been building up inside your body and direct this towards that person. Hope that they will come to understand the reasons for your initial anger and resentment so that they can amend their behaviour and are less likely to offend others in the future. Now let go of all the anger and resentment that you have been fostering towards this person, and instead feel nothing but good will and kindness towards them. Visualise them in your mind's eye and imagine them becoming surrounded by a blue light as your forgiveness envelops them. Once you are sure that you no longer feel anything towards that person but good will and forgiveness then that part of the meditation is complete.

Now it is time to think of someone that you have offended or harmed in some way and whose forgiveness you require. This can be something that has happened recently or even something far in the past that you still suffer guilt over. Hope that they are aware

of the reasons for your actions and also for the guilt
that they have caused you. Hope that you have learnt
from your mistakes and are unlikely to repeat them in
the future. Now let go of any feelings of guilt that this
mistake has caused you to suffer. It is time to forgive
yourself for your mistakes. When you feel that you
have replaced all negative feelings of bitterness and
resentment with a feeling of forgiveness then you can
end the meditation.

7   Devotional Meditation

Do not be put off by the title of this meditation.
Although it requires some religious belief and is not
suitable for atheists, it is not necessary to be of any
particular religious persuasion to practise this, and it is
suitable for people of all religious persuasions. When I
refer to 'God' during this meditation, I am not just
referring to the figurehead of Christianity but am using
this as a shorthand way to refer to all Gods of all
religions.

Meditation and prayer can be seen as very similar
practices. Both can be used as a way of achieving
communication with God. The main difference
between the two is that often during prayer, we tend to
ask for things that we do not have or strongly desire.
Although there is nothing stopping us from praying for
other people during prayer, this tends to be secondary
to praying for ourselves, and our own needs, whether
these be real or imagined. Thus prayer can often be

seen as a selfish practise. Meditation tends to be more neutral as many non-religious people practise it and while many people feel that it brings them nearer to God, this does not tend to be so they can pray for their own desires to be fulfilled. It is more likely to be in order to send out love, compassion and forgiveness to others. Praying or meditating in a selfless manner is usually considered to be more beneficial to the soul.

In order to practise the devotional meditation, you should first find a suitable place. You can choose somewhere sacred like a church or as with any other meditation you can simply practise it in your own home. Now choose a suitable position. You can choose to kneel with your hands clasped in front of you, or you can choose any of the positions that you would normally use during a meditation.

Now relax and take regular, deep breaths. Focus on your breathing for a few minutes. Now say a prayer for yourself inwardly and silently. This can be anything – a prayer that you would normally say at a church service or even one that you have made up yourself. This prayer can also be addressed to any God or Gods that you believe in. Once you have said a prayer for yourself, say one for someone else. This can be someone who is close to you or even an acquaintance you barely know – as long as the prayer is selfless, it doesn't matter who it is for. Now say a prayer for the entire universe and everyone in it. Say each prayer a few times each. If you catch yourself praying selfishly then simply acknowledge the fact and then let it go. It is a waste of energy to dwell on this – energy that could be better spent praying for others.

The more you practise this meditation, the less selfish you will be as an individual and the more spiritually evolved you will become.

8 Light Meditation

This is a Buddhist meditation that uses visualisation of light as a focus. The light symbolises a positive life force and fills the entire body leaving it cleansed, purified and invigorated.

In order to practise this meditation, select a suitable environment and position in which to meditate and close the eyes. Breathe evenly and deeply for a few moments until you become relaxed but alert. Now imagine that there is a small circle of light in the space just above your head. Imagine this circle of light as being about 10 to 15 centimetres above the top of your head. Focus on this light for a few minutes. It should appear as a bright, translucent circle. Concentrate on the bright, radiant energy this light is giving off. Think of this light as symbolising everything that is positive in this world, such as love, compassion, generosity of spirit, and kindness towards others. Continue to focus on this light for a few more minutes. If you have trouble visualising it, it does not matter too much. As long as you are aware of its presence and the values that it symbolises, that will be enough in order to continue with this meditation.

As you focus on this circle of light, imagine it growing larger in diameter. It should continue to grow larger and larger until it bursts and begins to travel downwards. Now imagine this light begin to suffuse throughout your entire body, filling you with energy and radiance. Visualise this light surrounding your entire body and spread down through the crown of your head, through your face and down into your neck. Watch as it continues its journey into your shoulders and down into each arm until it reaches the tips of the fingers in each hand. Now, imagine it as it begins to spread throughout your upper body. Watch it spread down into your torso and into each breast, spreading down into the abdomen until your entire upper body and head is suffused with a radiant white light. Now watch it as it continues its journey down into your lower body. Imagine the light filling each buttock and then spreading down into each leg and each foot until it reaches the sole of the feet and the tips of the toes.

Visualise your entire body as begin filled with and surrounded by an aura of brilliant white light that carries with it all the positive values in the universe such as love and compassion. Imagine this light as a purifying energy replacing any negative emotions in the body with nothing but positive emotions. All negative energy should have evaporated from your body leaving behind nothing but positive radiant energy thus allowing you to reach your highest potential as a human being. After the meditation has finished, try to hold onto the feeling that you are surrounded by this positive aura. Imagine that by touching others you have the power to infuse them with the same positive life force.

9 Yin and Yang Meditation

This meditation focuses on the idea of balance that is present throughout nature. In our lives, we have a tendency to desire the positive without having to experience the negative – to receive the love of others without ever coming into contact with their hatred; to enjoy material wealth without ever knowing the sting of poverty. We delude ourselves that it is possible to experience the good without also experiencing the bad. We have already looked at the phenomena of Yin and Yang in the section on Taoism. Just to recap, these are the two opposing forces that the Chinese use to symbolise the balance or equilibrium that is present in all natural creations. While Yin and Yang remain in balance, there will be a sense of harmony. If one is allowed to out balance the other, then this will cause discordance until balance is once again restored.

As with Yin and Yang, it is important that we retain a sense of balance within ourselves. If we expect to experience pleasure then we also must accept that we will at some point experience pain. Indeed, it can be argued that the phenomenon of pleasure would not even exist were it not for its counterpart, pain. We can retain this sense of inner balance with meditation.

To practise the Yin and Yang meditation, first find a comfortable environment and position in which to meditate. Now begin to breathe slowly and regularly. Concentrate on your breathing until you feel a state of pure awareness coming on. Now turn your attention to your feelings. Think about how you have been feeling today. Has someone angered you in some way? Perhaps you have been feeling a little bit down or lacking in energy. Choose a negative emotion that you have been feeling recently and focus on this emotion for a few minutes. Think about what made you feel this way and cast your mind back to other occasions when you have felt like this.

Now in order to restore balance in your emotions, choose the very antithesis of the negative emotion that you have been experiencing. For example, if you have been feeling depressed then focus on feelings of buoyancy and exuberance. If you have been feeling lethargic, then focus on a feeling of energy and enthusiasm for life. If you have been feeling angry towards someone then turn this anger into feelings of forgiveness, compassion and good will towards that person. Whatever negative emotion you have experiencing, counteract this by focusing on a positive emotion. Meditate on this positive emotion for a few minutes until all traces of the negative emotion have gone, having been entirely replaced by its positive counterpart. Once this negative emotion has vanished, you can end the meditation. You will find that with regular practise, this meditation will allow you to be more positive in general in your daily life. Whenever you are tempted to react with anger, you will find that the mind will automatically turn to feelings of compassion and kindness in place of this anger.

10 Positive Thought Meditation

In chapter 9, we looked at the immense power of thought when it comes to changing our behaviour for the better. This positive thought meditation has a similar concept behind it to the meditations in chapter 9, but is a quicker more general meditation.

It would be interesting to count how many times you utter a negative statement or harbour a negative thought in the average day. You would more than likely be surprised at how often you do this as to react with negativity has become an almost automatic reaction for many of us. Negativity is very human emotion and is easy to slip into if we do not monitor our behaviour. It is also a huge waste of energy that could be put to better use in other ways. A negative response rarely does anyone any good and in fact is likely to make a situation even worse, whereas a positive response usually does much good. Think of the negative energy that we are constantly giving off with our negative reactions and how these could have an adverse effect on the lives and mental state of those people surrounding us.

To practise this meditation, choose a suitable place and position in which to meditate. Focus the attention on the breathing until you reach a state of conscious awareness. Now direct your attention to going over the events of the day, or, if it is in the morning, cast your mind back to the previous day. Think of an occasion where you were tempted to or actually did react in a negative manner. Think what thoughts prompted this negative action and what was going through your mind at the time. If you can understand the chain of events that led to your being negative, then it makes it easier to stop yourself from doing it again. Think what effect your reaction had both on the other people involved and on your own state of mind. Negativity breeds further negativity. Now think of a more positive way that you could have reacted. Think how much better this would have made everyone including yourself feel. Imagine how this positive frame of mind could have exerted a positive influence over other people that you met that day and over the rest of the events in that day.

Being negative is a hard habit to break and this meditation will require much practise before you start to notice results. If you catch yourself being negative, whether during the meditation or in everyday life, do not react with anger or disappointment, as this will only generate more negativity. Instead, simply acknowledge the negative thought and then replace it with a more positive thought. You will start to find that at first your behaviour will become more positive as you will catch yourself before you are about to make a negative action. Then with more practice you will find that your very thoughts become more positive in general. Negative things happens to us all but it is the way in which we react to them that determines whether or not they are a completely negative experience or whether we are able to learn something from them and therefore turn them into a positive experience.

CHAPTER 13
Chakras and Meditation

Ancient Indian Yogic literature describes special energy centres in our bodies called chakras. Chakra is the Sanskrit word for wheel and chakras are said to appear to those who can see them as spinning wheels of light. Chakras can be found in the aura – an electromagnetic forcefield which proponents of chakra meditation believe to surround every living creature. Chakras are said to connect our physical and spiritual bodies. The aura is said to be the collective energy produced by our thoughts and feelings and each chakra exists at one of the points of the human body where this energy is most concentrated. The chakras are believed to maintain their supply of energy from the life force that is believed to be present all around us, and the energy concentrated in this chakra is also said to flow throughout through the body in order to nourish each part.

Each chakra is connected to a specific endocrine gland and all the chakras are connected to one another. The chakras are also said to relate to specific organs in the body. The health of each organ depends on whether or not the chakra is successfully spinning or not. When all of our chakras are open, spinning, bright, and clean then our system is balanced. Our chakras can become blocked if, for example, we are suffering from stress of some kind of emotional problem, abusing substances or failing to exercise properly. When the chakras become blocked, there is said to be a disruption in the flow of energy throughout the body. This is believed to lead to physical illness, disease and psychological and emotional problems. The person will also start to exhibit problems in the area that the blocked chakra is thought to be connected to. It is thought to be possible to keep your chakras balanced and vibrating effectively by regular meditation sessions. In keeping your chakras balanced, you will ensure that there is no disruption in the flow of energy throughout the body and that each part of your mental and physical constitution will remain in a state of equilibrium – rather like the Chinese concept of Yin and Yang. It is also believed that meditating regularly on the chakras will not only keep them balanced, but will also allow you to reach a higher level of consciousness.

Each chakra is also said to be connected to a number of stones or crystals. Because of their molecular structure, crystals are thought to radiate a flow of energy. These stones can be incorporated into the chakra meditations as they are said to be useful in helping to balance the chakras. This is done by balancing an appropriate stone on top of the chakra that you feel you are experiencing problems with. This helps to open the chakra an allow it to start spinning freely again. Many people determine whether a chakra is working or not by swinging a pendulum over that area and seeing if it spins properly.

There are many different theories regarding the number of and location of chakras, but the most common theory is that there are seven. It is thought that there is a current of energy that flows vertically through the body down the spine. These seven chakras are vertically aligned through the centre of the body and are therefore positioned along this line of power.

These seven chakras are as follows:

1. The Root or Base Chakra

The root chakra is located at the base of the spine and those who claim to be able to see the chakras say that it emanates a black, brown or red light. This chakra said to be at the root of our existence and is therefore has the most disrupting influence when blocked or unbalanced. It is necessary to have a steady base on which to build, so it is vital that we pay extra attention to our base chakra to maintain good health in every area. It is also associated with material life.

When balanced and operating efficiently, this chakra links our spiritual and physical selves. It allows us to enjoy our existence in the physical world and feel at one with our bodies. This chakra is also said to be able to enhance the link between our past and present.

It can help us glean the wisdom from past experiences so that we can then apply this wisdom to present situations. It also helps us to let go of any negative feelings or fear we may have due to bad experiences in the past.

This chakra is associated with the colour red. Red shows the link that the root chakra has to the Earth, the trees and all of nature's creations. Red can be seen to represent fire and consumption. A healthy root chakra is believed to consume negativity and doubt, allowing you to grab a hold of life with both hands.

When your root chakra is blocked then you lack a sense of stability regarding your existence in the world, and you will also become prone to worrying about money and social status. An unbalanced root chakra may also lead to problems with parts of your anatomy, including your bladder, colon, and lower back.

In order to maintain a healthy root chakra, there are meditations that can be performed. See the end of this chapter for a meditation that balances all of the chakras. There are also physical activities that can be performed in order to energise each chakra. Dancing, drumming, and just about any other activity that involves music are particularly good activities for imbuing the root chakra with positive healing energy.

CRYSTALS ASSOCIATED WITH THE ROOT CHAKRA
• *Black Tourmaline*: This stone imbues you with a sense of protection and stops you feeling threatened.

- *Hematite*: This stone helps to create a sense of space and privacy, and is useful when you are feeling claustrophobic in the company of others.
- *Tiger's Eye*: This is perhaps the most suitable crystal for meditating on the base chakra as it enhances your sense of physicality.
- *Smoky Quartz*: This stone is said to connect the root chakra with the crown chakra, promoting the flow of energy throughout the body and increasing your holistic sense of wellbeing.

These crystals should be placed at the base of the spine during meditation.

2. The Sacral Chakra

This chakra is said to be located in the genital area just above the pelvic bone. The sacral chakra is associated with the energy flow through the body and more particularly with the sexual and creative energy. It represents passion and a feeling of lust for life. It is important that too much emphasis is not placed on the sexual associations of this chakra as the passion that it radiates can be for creative and artistic pursuits as well as for sex. It also carries a strong association with the five senses.

When this chakra is balanced and functioning efficiently, we feel a general sense of wellbeing and joie de vivre. We are full of energy and enjoy spontaneous activities. We are highly creative, open and expressive.

When this chakra becomes blocked or unbalanced, we develop low self-esteem, we may feel unattractive and our sex drive can become adversely affected.

This chakra is also associated with our feelings of masculinity or femininity, and our sense of these can become undermined when the chakra stops to function effectively. Our source of creativity dries up and we become less open and spontaneous. The physical consequences of a blocked or unbalanced sacral chakra can include disease of the reproductive organs, stiffness in the hips, and kidney problems.

This chakra is associated with the colour orange, which is a strong vibrant colour that conveys a sense of creativity and passion. When we wear a bright colour like orange, we become more self-confident and full of energy. Visualising the orange light of the sacral chakra during meditation will energise the chakra as well as making you feel a sense of joy and freedom.

As this chakra represents creative passion, any creative activity is effective in helping to energise this chakra. Particularly recommended are painting, drawing and writing.

CRYSTALS ASSOCIATED WITH THE SACRAL CHAKRA
- *Bloodstone*: This stone is effective in increasing your energy levels.
- *Carnelian*: This stone promotes creativity and helps to banish indecision.
- *Red Garnet*: This crystal is said to imbue you with a sense of patience.

- *Red Jasper*: This stone is supposed to enhance your connection with the energy that flows through the Earth and is therefore also suitable for use with the root chakra.
- *Ruby*: This stone is believed to represent passion and is suitable for arousing the senses.
- *Rose*: This stone is said to provide gentle, loving energy that heals the sacral chakra.

These stones should be placed above the pelvic bone when meditating on the sacral chakra.

3. The Solar Plexus Chakra

The solar plexus chakra is located in the diaphragm and is associated with physical and material power. This chakra has particular influence on the physical world and can help us to remain determined whilst realising our goals and potential. It also enhances our sense of individuality.

When this chakra is unblocked and functioning properly, we are aware of our own self-worth. We feel full of confidence and conviction and are free to pursue our aims and goals without any nagging doubts. We do not try and bully others, nor do we sacrifice our own beliefs because others disagree with them. We associate with people who accept us the way that we are and do not attempt to change any part of us. Tending to this chakra in particular will help us to stay focussed, stay true to our own beliefs, and help us to pursue our dreams.

When blocked, this chakra can render us full of self-doubt and indecision. This can leave us vulnerable to being bullied and pushed around. We begin to dwell upon problems and worry about what the future may bring. Alternatively, it can make us overestimate our sense of power and become bullying and aggressive. We can start to surround ourselves with people that we recognise as being weaker so that we are able to control them all the more and disguise our own feelings of inadequacy.

The physical problems associated with a blocked solar plexus chakra include stomach ulcers, indigestion, a sluggish digestive system and a tendency to abuse substances such as drugs and alcohol. An unbalanced solar plexus chakra can also contribute to eating disorders can either lead us to begin to deprive ourselves of food or start to overindulge in order to block out a sense of failure caused by a lack of volition.

The solar plexus chakra is associated with the colour yellow. This colour represents a sense of vibrancy, optimism and energy. Often just begin surrounded by the colour yellow can give us a mental lift. Just think of a time when you have gone out for a walk on a bright, sunny day and have returned feeling more positive than when you began. Wearing this colour can give off an impression of confidence and a sense of individuality.

Activities that can help to energise the solar plexus chakra include those that include gentle movement such as walking and swimming. It is also said to be helpful to drink lots of water and include many vegetables in your diet if you wish to cleanse the solar plexus chakra.

CRYSTALS ASSOCIATED WITH THE SOLAR PLEXUS CHAKRA

- *Aragonite*: This crystal is believed to calm and stabilise particularly where the emotions are concerned.
- *Citrine*: This stone is said to be good for the will and can boost your sense of determination.
- *Golden Calcite*: This crystal is effective when used to enhance your sense of energy, particularly in personal relationships.
- *Malachite*: This stone is especially good for clearing the solar plexus chakra and enhances your sense of creativity.
- *Rhodochrosite*: This crystal is said to be good for aiding correct breathing and is therefore appropriate for many forms of meditation.
- *Rutilated Quartz*: This stone is also good for enhancing creativity, especially when realising dreams.
- *Pyrite*: Also a stone to be used for enhancing creativity.
- *Unakite*: This stone provides an aid in understanding mental and emotional problems. It also allows us to pinpoint and remove conditions that have been hindering our personal growth.

These crystals should be places above the diaphragm – the area of the abdomen that moves up and down as we breathe – when meditating on the solar plexus chakra.

4. The Heart Chakra

This chakra is located in the chest and is level with the heart. It is connected to our feelings of love and emotional stability. When functioning properly, we feel a sense of goodwill towards others and are attracted to people who are likely to return our love and respect. This chakra is also said to govern the heart and lungs. These are the most vital parts of our physical selves as the lungs are responsible for supplying oxygen, which the heart then pumps around the body, supplying this vital oxygen to all the organs in the body. Without this supply of oxygen, we would die.

When this chakra is unbalanced, we have difficulty forming relationships with others and may maintain grudges against them as we find it difficult to forgive those who we feel have betrayed us or let us down in some way. Physical problems accompanying a blocked heart chakra include problems with the heart, stiffness in the shoulders or back and respiratory problems such as asthma.

The heart chakra is said to be green. This colour represents nature – the source of all life and creation.

It is a cool, calm colour that can soothe a troubled mind, and it helps to remind us of our connection to all living things.

Activities that are supposed to help energise the heart chakra include music, yoga and any form of self-expression. Walking in the countryside is also particularly effective for energising the heart chakra.

CRYSTALS ASSOCIATED WITH THE HEART CHAKRA

- *Aventurine*: This stone is related to physical health, especially the health of the heart.
- *Emerald*: This stone is believed to relate to the spiritual component of love.
- *Green calcite*: This stone helps to remove old, unproductive ideas, allowing more room for new, fresh ideas.
- *Green tourmaline*: This stone allows us to connect our emotions and our creativity.
- *Lepidolite*: This helps to calm the heart and soothe a troubled mind.
- *Rose Quartz*: This stone is vital in the promotion of unconditional self-love - an emotion that is necessary for self-fulfilment.

These crystals should be placed in the middle of the chest when meditating on the heart chakra.

5. The Throat Chakra

This chakra is located in the throat and is associated with communication and mental power. When it is unblocked and vibrating freely, we are able to articulate ourselves, and relay messages to others with no difficulty. This means that we also become more assertive as we have less difficulty in conveying more taboo emotions such as anger and annoyance.

When this chakra is not functioning properly we have a great deal of difficulty in communicating and in helping others to see our point of view. We are also inhibited when it comes to expressing our sense of creativity. We can become shy and introverted. Or this process can become inverted and we become overbearing and loud in an attempt to disguise our feelings of inadequacy. Either way, our real sense is being prevented from emerging.

In contemporary western society, it is common for people to experience a blockage in the throat chakra. Physical problems of this blockage can include eating disorders as people can often turn to food for comfort when they are feeling cut off through a lack of communication with others. Other problems can include respiratory diseases, toothache, gun disease and any other problem to do with the mouth or throat.

This chakra is supposed to be linked to the colour turquoise or pale blue. As the colour of the sea and sky, blue also reminds us of our connection to nature. It also imbues us with a sense of freedom in its connection with such fluid elements as water and air. It is a calming, tranquil colour that soothes the mind and can be seen to represent wisdom – a vital component of successful communication.

The activity most recommended for energising the

throat chakra is song and poetry. These activities celebrate the gifts of communication and self-expression that we possess. When we sing or recite, the vibrations created travel through our entire bodies clearing away blockages in the flow of energy that travels to and from each chakra. Nothing has such as uplifting effect as music. This effect can be reinforced if you select a song that has lyrics which are particularly meaningful to you.

CRYSTALS ASSOCIATED WITH THE THROAT CHAKRA

- *Angelite*: This stone is effective in eliminating anger and is also good for promoting a connection with a higher consciousness.
- *Aquamarine*: This helps you to express yourself without resorting to anger.
- *Turquoise*: This stone increases your powers of persuasion.
- *Blue lace agate*: This stone can help you to realise your potential for accomplishment.
- *Blue topaz*: This stone is said to enhance creativity and also to add conviction to your communications.
- *Celestite*: This stone encourages you to be receptive to the ideas of others and also calms the thoughts.

These crystals should be placed in the hollow on the neck just above the throat when meditating on the throat chakra.

6. The Third Eye Chakra

This chakra is located just between the eyebrows and is associated with psychic ability including intuition and religious awareness. On a physical level, it governs the senses and the pituitary glands, the skull, the eyes, the brain and the nervous system.

If this chakra is vibrating healthily, we remain in touch with our psychic as well as our physical powers. We can interpret our dreams and use them to direct us in our worldly lives and can trust our sense of instinct and intuition when making decisions. Our sense of wisdom remains intact, something that is necessary if we are to achieve enlightenment.

When this chakra is blocked, we become fearful of any psychic ability that we possess and try to block out unpleasant dreams rather than trying to get to the crux of what other problems or worries have caused them. The physical symptoms associated with a blocked third eye chakra include blocked sinuses, earache, insomnia and anxiety.

This chakra is associated with purple. Purple is a colour that is believed to enhance our spirituality and creativity. It is also said to stimulate the brain to absorb new information.

Activities that are said to energise the third eye chakra are meditation and listening to mood music. Anything that engages the brain, helping to keep us focussed whilst rendering us relaxed is good for this chakra.

CRYSTALS ASSOCIATED WITH THE THIRD EYE CHAKRA

- *Amethyst*: This stone is said to aid sleep and encourage pleasant dreams.
- *Azurite*: This crystal encourages us to examine old beliefs and discard those that are no longer relevant.
- *Lapus lazuli*: This is similar to the azurite as it helps us to pinpoint hidden beliefs that are determining our behaviour.
- *Moss agate*: This stone is said to balance both the hemispheres of the brain to encourage a balance of emotions and other mental functions.

These crystals should be placed between the eyebrows when meditating on the third eye chakra.

7. The Crown Chakra

The crown chakra can be found at the crown of the head and is connected to the spiritual universe. When it is balanced and functioning properly, we feel a sense of connection with the universe and understand our place within it. We lose the existentialist belief that we are somehow separate from other people and other natural creations. We are all components of the one universe and it is possible to enjoy a feeling of individuality at the same time as recognising ourselves as one part of a whole.

When this chakra is failing to function properly, we feel lonely and isolated from others. We may also envy others and feel that we do not measure up to them. We also have morbid thoughts and fear death. Physical problems associated with a blocked crown chakra include headaches, nervous problems and outbreaks of acne.

As the crown chakra has such strong ties with spirituality, any activity that attempts to engage with a higher consciousness is suitable for practising in order to energise this chakra. Particularly recommended are meditation, yoga and reiki.

The crown chakra is associated with the colour white. White can be seen to represent power and a holistic sense of wellbeing as it is made up of all the other colours together. White can also be seen as a symbol of purity and by visualising this light emanating from our crown chakras, we can start to feel cleansed.

CRYSTALS ASSOCIATED WITH THE CROWN CHAKRA

- *Clear calcite*: This stone is said to relieve our problems with a spiritual understanding.
- *Herkimer*: This crystal is said to radiate more light and energy that other stones and is therefore particularly good at dissolving blockages.
- *Diamond*: Like the herkimer, the diamond is a particularly radiant stone and is therefore good at balancing chakras.
- *Danburite*: This stone is said to enhance our sense of spirituality and can imbue us with a sense of calmness even in the face of adversity.

These crystals should be allowed to rest against the crown of the head when meditating on the crown chakra.

The seven main chakras and their various attributes can be summarised in the following table:

Chakra	Location/Colour	Associations
The Root or Base Chakra	Base of spine/ Red	Our sense of physicality Money/security worries Symbolises a connection with the Earth
The Sacral Chakra	Genital area/ Orange	Sexuality and desire Health of lower body
The Solar Plexus Chakra	Diaphragm/ Yellow	Sense of power Addictions Digestive system Metabolism
The Heart Chakra	Chest/ Green	Capacity for love Anger, resentment, forgiveness

Related region of anatomy	Crystal/Stone	Mantra
Bladder, colon, adrenal glands Spine, lower back Blood, bone, immune system	Black Tourmaline Hematite Tiger's Eye Smoky Quartz	Lam
Reproductive organs, hips, lower abdomen, spleen, kidneys, prostate	Bloodstone Carnelian Red Garnet Red Jasper Ruby	Vam
Stomach, intestines, pancreas, liver, gall bladder, back	Aragonite Citrine Golden Calcite Malachite Rhodochrosite Rutilated Quartz Pyrite Unakite	Ram
Thymus gland, lymph glands, lungs, heart, circulation, breasts, back, shoulders and arms	Aventurine Emerald Green calcite Green tourmaline Lepidolite Rose Quartz	Yam

Chakra	Location/Colour	Associations
The Throat Chakra	Throat/ Blue, turquoise	Communicative skills Creativity, expression
The Third-Eye or Brow Chakra	Centre of forehead/ Purple	Psychic abilities Visions and dreams Religious consciousness
Crown Chakra	Crown of head/ white	Spirituality Sense of peace, wellbeing

Meditating On the Chakras

There are many ways that you can meditate on the chakras in order to ensure that they are balanced and functioning properly. One way that is recommended for unblocking chakras but not for overactive ones is projecting love and light into the chakras. This is done by first selecting the chakra that you wish to unblock and visualising a brilliant white light flowing into that chakra. This light represents love and a healing,

212

Related region of anatomy	Crystal/Stone	Mantra
Thyroid gland, parathyroid, larynx, throat, tongue, mouth, teeth Eating disorders	Angelite Aquamarine Turquoise Blue lace agate Blue topaz Celestite	Ham
Sinuses, ears and eyes Insomnia Anxiety	Amethyst Azurite Lapus lazuli Moss agate	Om (short)
Brain, cerebral cortex, pituitary gland, nervous system, skin	Clear calcite Herkimer Diamond Danburite	Om (long)

cleansing energy. Imagine this light flowing into the troublesome chakra, healing it and restoring it to its proper function.

This is an effective meditation as it allows you to target the specific area that you wish to treat. For example, if you are having difficulty in communicating then you can imagine this light flowing into the throat chakra and healing it, thus rendering you a more articulate person, better equipped to express your thoughts and beliefs. It is also useful when treating a particular chakra to repeat the mantra that is associated with that chakra (see the above table).

Perhaps the most effective way to meditate on the chakras is to perform a general meditation that balances all of the chakras at the same time. In order to perform this chakra balancing meditation, first select from the list above at least one crystal for each chakra. Choose one that you feel you could benefit most from. This is a good meditation to perform as it balances all the chakras, including those that you did not even know were unbalanced. Lie down on your back – if you wish, you can use a mat for added comfort – and place at least one crystal on its corresponding chakra.

Take deep slow breaths. Imagine the air flowing down through your body, following the direction of the channel of energy that runs from the crown of your head to the base of your spine.

After you have been doing this exercise for some minutes and are starting to feel alert awareness, you can begin to meditate on each chakra. Travelling from the crown to the root chakra, visualise each one as it swirls around. Look at the beautiful colours of each chakra. If you wish to focus on a particular chakra, you can speak to it either by repeating the mantra for that particular chakra or by reciting an affirmation to that chakra. For example, if you wish to work on your ability to forgive and rid yourself of a particular grudge you are carrying, then you can try speaking directly to the heart chakra. Imagine yourself emanating a green light and repeat the affirmation, 'I feel a sense of love and goodwill towards all other people and forms of life.' Feel all those feelings of resentment and bitterness melt away, and feel your body become filled with love and kindness towards other people and towards yourself.

This is an effective meditation to perform as it has all the benefits of a normal meditation and ensures that all your chakras remain balanced, even if you were unaware that they were blocked or unbalanced to begin with. As you become more adept at this meditation, it is said that you will find that you are more able to anticipate your chakras becoming unbalanced and can prevent this from happening in the first place.

CHAPTER 14
Disciplines which Complement Meditation

When taking up meditation, it is important that you are aware of the many other practices there are which can complement it. I have chosen to briefly discuss those that I feel can have the most benefit when combined with regular meditation, but there are many more alternative practices and therapies available for you to try. Do not be afraid to experiment.

Yoga

The practise of yoga is very similar to meditation and often you will find that the two terms are used interchangeably in certain books. Yoga is a spiritual discipline that originated in India 2,500 years ago and was connected to the religions of Buddhism, Hinduism and Jainism. Along with meditation, yoga is said to exist as the final branch of the Buddhist eight-fold path to nirvana. The popularity of yoga has increased in recent years not only due to the increased popularity and mainstream acceptance of New Age philosophy, but also due to the increased interest in health and fitness techniques.

In the West, we tend to think of yoga as simply being about the positions or asanas that are associated with yoga but in fact this is only one part of a more complicated discipline. This form of yoga is known as hatha yoga and it was not developed until long after yoga was established in India some 2,500 years ago. The original form of hatha yoga involved techniques of breath control and thousands of different postures. It is a difficult form of yoga that was originally designed to strengthen the body and release latent energy in order to make the body more powerful for worship.

Yoga shares many goals with meditation including the pursuit of enlightenment, happiness and freedom, and is a practise that actually incorporates meditation. Yoga has many other benefits that are said to be achieved along the way including physical health, mental harmony and emotional stability. Practised in its truest form, yoga, like meditation, is said to help us unlock our full potential as human beings. Like meditation, yoga started as a means of connecting with a greater spiritual power and of transcending the mundane existence of daily life. The word yoga is Sankrit for 'union', which reflects the goal of practising yoga. Like meditation, yoga originated as a lifestyle concerned with a holistic approach to health and good living that promoted a sense of unity between the physical and mental self. People who chose to take up yoga had to follow a number of rules which eventually led to them achieving a connection with a higher spiritual consciousness. These rules are outlined below and are referred to as the Eight-Fold Path:

1. Yamas: These are rules that are intended to eliminate our base instincts.
2. Niyamas: These are rules that are intended to improve upon our individual personalities.
3. Asanas: These are the postures that most people in the West have come to associate with yoga. They are followed in order to gain control over the body.
4. Pranayama: This is a method of learning to control the breath.
5. Pratyahara: This is the withdrawal from the five senses.
6. Dharana: This is the development of concentration.
7. Dhyana: This is meditation.
8. Samadhi: The final stage in the eight-fold path is the union with a higher consciousness.

The Yamas and Niyamas are summarised below:

YAMAS
- Abstinence from violence of any kind.
- Abstinence from lying.
- Abstinence from stealing.
- Chastity.
- Practise of moderation and avoidance of greed.

NIYAMAS
- Cleanliness in body and mind.
- Contentment with one's lot.
- Practising austerity.
- Self-improvement.
- A commitment to seeking nirvana or the ultimate truth

As you can see, this was a very demanding set of rules and few people have ever managed to follow all of the rules and achieved enlightenment or a connection with a higher consciousness. The later rules required that the individual become completely isolated from life and go and in a secluded monastery. This was impossible for those people who had families to support, which were the vast majority in those days, and so few people were able to complete the eightfold path.

In today's hectic society, it is even less practical for people to go and live in seclusion and withdraw from sensory stimuli. This is why most forms of yoga, like most forms of meditation, only require that the practitioner give up a certain amount of time per week rather than having to make drastic changes to his or her lifestyle. In the West, most yoga classes are mainly concerned with a version of hatha yoga – that is, mastering the asanas and with achieving a fit and supple body. Some classes teach softer versions of this yoga that are concerned with suppleness and relaxation and are suitable for untrained bodies. Like meditation, yoga is not necessarily a physically demanding practice and so people of any age and level of fitness can practise it. There are, however, more energetic courses for those who want more of an aerobic workout. There are also many videos available providing introductory courses although most experts recommend that you attend a class with a trained instructor to begin with in order to avoid potential injuries. Unlike meditation, with yoga there is a chance that you could injure yourself by forming an asana incorrectly.

If you are not interested in the physical side of yoga, there are other approaches that you can take which have been developed by various gurus. For example, there are classes available in yoga that involves intellectual rather than physical activity, classes that involve the use of visual and aural stimuli, and classes that concentrate more on the meditative aspect of yoga.

The following styles of yoga are said to complement the practice of meditation particularly well:

Ananda

Ananda yoga is a style of hatha yoga developed by Swami Kriyananda that was designed in order to prepare the body for meditation. This style of yoga uses postures and breathing techniques to relax the body whilst exploring the consciousness. It places particularly energy on energising the chakras, something that we looked at in chapter 13. The objective of ananda yoga is to create a sense of balance within the self and to achieve a connection with a higher level of consciousness. One feature that is exclusive to the practice of ananda yoga is to inwardly repeat affirmations while in the asanas. This is a gentle form of yoga that is more suited to exploring the consciousness and relaxing the body rather than being geared towards a work out.

Integral

Integral yoga is a style of yoga developed by Swami Satchidananda. It places emphasis on breathing techniques and meditation, as well as on the more commonly used asanas. Yoga experts recommend this yoga to those people who have a weak heart.

Kripalu

Inspired by Kripalvananda, Kripalu yoga is also known as the yoga of consciousness. This form of yoga places great emphasis on breathing techniques, correct alignment of the body and the co-ordination of breathing and movement. In Kripalu yoga, students focus their attention on the feeling that is produced by adopting various postures, a technique that is believed to develop their mind, body and spirit. This form of yoga is broken down into three stages. Stage one consists of learning the correct postures and exploring the capability of the body. Stage two consists of maintaining these postures for extended periods of time whilst developing conscious awareness. The third and final stage is concerned with a form of meditation in which the individual is seen to move from one posture to another as a series of unconscious and spontaneous actions.

Kundalini

Kundalini yoga is a very traditional form of yoga that was originally brought to the West by Yogi Bhajanin the late sixties. This form of yoga is said to assist the release of Kundalini energy. This involves learning postures, breathing techniques, chanting, co-ordinating breath and movement and meditation.

Viniyoga

Created by Shri Krishnamacharya, Viniyoga is not a singular style of yoga, but it is a methodology that has been developed in order to create tailor made practices for individuals that suit their specific needs. Each practise is created in order to adhere to the needs of the individual and can include breathing techniques, postures and meditation. This is normally taught on a one-to one basis.

Like meditation, there are many benefits to be gleaned from the regular practise of yoga. After you have been attending classes for a few weeks you will no doubt start to feel increasingly fit and supple with reduced levels of stress. If you continue practising yoga for a significant length of time, you will notice further benefits still and not only benefits of a physical nature. It is said that practising yoga on a long-term basis leads to dramatic improvements in general health, increased confidence, increased sense of mental well being and increased ability to cope with stressful situations. Proponents of yoga have also reported that they have become more forthright, assertive and purposeful people since taking up the practise. Like meditation, practising yoga is also said to help people give up addictions like smoking and drinking.

Even if we chose not to pursue spiritual advancement, the practise of yoga can still allow us to transcend petty, day-to-day concerns and become more calm, stable people. As with meditation, yoga can increase our sense of self-awareness and make us more sensitive people. This can also improve or relationships with others as we become more laid-back caring people and also more acceptable of other people's faults. Like proponents of meditation, proponents of yoga also believe that in our stressful hectic, society we have lost touch with our values and with who we really are. The increased interest in working-out and personal grooming in recent years shows that people are yearning for something that will transport them beyond the banality of everyday life. What they do not realise is that the thing that they are missing is not to be acquired through manipulating their external appearance or through physical exertion, but through exploring their inner self.

Yogic Breathing Techniques

Yogic breathing or pranayama is the fourth limb in the eight-fold path to enlightenment. We have already touched upon the importance of correct breathing when meditating and the same holds true for yoga. In yoga, as with meditation, it is believed that to control the breathing is to control the mind and yoga has many techniques for doing so. The main techniques are listed below. When practised regularly, you will find that these techniques for breathing will also enhance your meditative sessions.

Complete Breath

We have previously discussed the tendency we have of only using the top portion of our lungs when we breathe and taking very shallow breaths. Proper yogic breathing incorporates each lung to its fullest capacity. This form of breathing is particularly effective as it teaches you how to breathe properly and this is beneficial to the health.

- To carry out proper breathing, first assume a comfortable position. A seated position is the most suitable for this exercise.
- Now draw in your abdominal muscles and push the air out of the bottom of the lungs. Relax the abdominal muscles.

- Now inhale slowly and deeply, filling the bottom of the lungs with air. Your abdomen will rise as you do so. Continue filling the middle section of the lungs, causing the rib cage to expand to its fullest capacity. Now continuing your inhalation, fill the top section of the lungs, causing the area below the collarbone to rise.
- Now exhale slowly feeling the air leave each part of your lungs. Do not inhale again until you are sure that your lungs are empty.

Cleansing Breath (*Ha Breath*)

This form of breathing is said to be most effective when standing. It is particularly effective for ensuring that the lungs are emptied properly, ridding them of any stale air that may be lurking there. It is also recommended for people who suffer from respiratory problems.

- First of all, stand with your feet slightly apart.
- Now inhale so that your lungs reach their fullest capacity. At the same time, lift your arms up past your sides and above your head.
- Now exhale and at the same time bend forward at the waist and make a 'ha' sound. Bending your knees slightly, swing your arms through your legs and pull in your tummy muscles in order to squeeze every last drop of air out of your lungs. Make sure that you have fully exhaled.
- Now inhale deeply and straighten you back whilst

simultaneously lifting your arms high above your head again.
- Repeat five times.

Alternative Nostril Breathing (Nadi Sodana)

This breathing technique is said to be particularly effective for alleviating anxiety, calming the mind and preventing insomnia. It is most effective when practised in a seated position.
- First of all, ensure you are sitting comfortably in an upright position with a straight spine.
- Now fold the index and middle finger of your right hand into your palm. Keep the thumb, the fourth finger and the pinkie straight.
- With your thumb, close your right nostril. Inhale deeply through the left nostril.
- Now with your pinkie and fourth finger close the left nostril and exhale through the right. Now inhale deeply through the right nostril.
- Repeat this process for a few minutes, inhaling and exhaling through alternate nostrils.

Bellows Breath (Bhastrika)

The Bellows Breath is particularly effective for promoting good circulation and clearing sinuses. It is also said to cleanse and invigorate the entire body. It is most suitably practised in a seated position.
- First of all, inhale deeply, filling the lungs to their

fullest capacity.
- Now exhale with as much force as you can muster, using the abdominal muscles to squeeze out every last particle of air.
- Now relax your abdominal muscles and allow the lungs to automatically fill up.
- Repeat this powerful exhalation, followed by an automatic inhalation.
- Practice this technique for a few minutes.

Bee Breath (Brahmari)

Bee Breath is said to help cure insomnia and to relax the body. This technique is best performed when seated.
- Firstly, close you eyes. And inhale slowly and deeply through the nostrils.
- Now as you exhale, make a low, humming sound like a bee. The sound should end when you finish exhaling.
- Inhale again, slowly and deeply.
- Now exhale and make the humming sound again. Focus on that sound.
- Continue this practise for a few minutes.

This breathing technique is suitable to be practised during meditation as it gives the mind an object to focus on.

Cooling Breath (*Sitali*)

The Cooling Breath technique is effective for relaxing the mind and body. It is also said to be good for the digestion system. This technique is most effective when performed seated or lying down.

- First of all, take deep slow breaths.
- Now curl up the sides of your tongue so that it forms a long tubular shape.
- Inhale slowly and deeply through your curled up tongue. The air will feel cool against your tongue.
- Now close your mouth and exhale through your nose.
- Repeat this for a few minutes.

Alexander Technique

It can be highly beneficial to study the Alexander Technique as you learn to meditate and many experts in meditation recommend this. Although the two practices have very different origins, they both involve correct breathing and posture. Practising one can therefore promote efficiency in the other. I will give a brief outline of the Alexander Technique here, but if you have the time then it is worth looking into further.

Unlike meditation, the Alexander Technique did not originate as a religious practise but was developed in the 19th century by an Australian man called Frederick Matthius Alexander. Alexander was born in 1869. He was the first of ten children and his parents owned a farmed in Tasmania. He was a sickly child and suffered from respiratory problems in particular. Instead of taking to the life on the farm, he became passionately interested in the arts – particularly the theatre. When in his late teens, he left the farm and went off to work in an office in a mining company. He soon found that he disliked this occupation and decided instead to become a professional reciter in the theatre. This meant that he single-handedly read out various plays to an audience.

Alexander was not working in this field for very long before he earned a reputation as a respected teacher of elocution. But something would happen to threaten this new-found success. The respiratory problems of Alexander's childhood came back to haunt him. He found that during recitals, speech would become more and more difficult and his voice would often disappear completely by the end of the performance. The people in the audience were also highly aware of these problems, as they would witness him struggling to breathe during performances. On seeking expert advice for this problem, he was told both by doctors and voice coaches that it was necessary for him to rest his vocal chords. He took this advice and did rest for a period. This did help, but whenever he went back to his work in the theatre, the problems would return. After this had happened several times, it occurred to Alexander that there must be a difference between the way he spoke during normal life and the way he spoke during a recital. He realised it was this difference that was causing the problem.

He finally established that this was due to the fact that he had a tendency to pull his head back, depressing his larynx, and inhale in a way that made him gasp. Once he had identified this as something he did during a performance, he soon discovered that he did it during daily life, too, although in a less emphatic manner. In fact, this breathing technique was always present but would only become obvious when Alexander was in a state of excitement or under stress in some way.

Alexander decided that this method of breathing was a habit that he had developed and could therefore be corrected. He set about trying to stop breathing in this way that was evidently causing him so many problems. However, when he attempted to stop pulling his head back before speaking, he found that he could not – this mode of behaviour was so established in his unconscious that it was all but impossible to correct. This is when he discovered inhibition – the cornerstone of his technique. He realised that if just before he spoke he inhibited the desire to speak and then instructed himself to lift his head forward and up, he could then overcome his old habit of putting his head back.

This method of inhibition is perhaps the most important aspect of the Alexander Technique. In order to correct ingrained and habitual behavioural patterns that have an adverse effect on health, it is first necessary to identify them. Then the desire to proceed with such a behavioural pattern can be inhibited and a less harmful mode of behaviour can be learned in its place.

Alexander started using this method of inhibition to correct his breathing technique. The improvement in both his breathing and his subsequent performances was so marked that other actors began to come to him for advice on similar problems. His reputation grew and grew and he was so successful at teaching others the technique he had formed that he decided to become a teacher for his career. His pupils came back to him to say that not only were their breathing patterns and delivery improved, but they also had an increased sense of wellbeing since learning Alexander's technique. His list of pupils then expanded to include people from all walks of life – not just from the world of theatre. Indeed, his reputation was so impressive that doctors began referring patients to him when all other forms of conventional medicine had failed them. This was when his brother, AR Alexander, became a partner in what was emerging as a successful business and while AR stayed in Melbourne to teach the technique, FM moved to Sydney to spread the benefits of this discovery even further afield.

As time went on, Alexander developed his technique to become the discipline that is taught all over the world today when he began to look at control of reactions in the body in general, not just in breathing and voice control. He wrote several pamphlets and four separate books on his technique. His theories were supported by several prominent and respected figures. For example, John Dewey, the famous American philosopher, came to Alexander for lessons. He then credited Alexander with having influenced much of his own work. Alexander realised that if his technique were to be universally recognised, he would need to establish a proper training course so that other people could learn and teach his principles. In 1931, the first teacher-training course in the Alexander Technique began.

The Alexander Technique is used in order to examine the way that we carry ourselves in our everyday activities. It looks at the way that we move, the way that we balance ourselves, the way we co-ordinate our movements and the way that we breathe. Like meditation, this technique has a holistic approach to health. It posits that certain bad habits we pick up can have an adverse effect on many different aspects of our health and in order to feel a general sense of wellbeing, it is necessary to find the source of the problem rather than just attempting to sure the symptom itself. This technique developed around the assumption that most of us have picked up several bad habits surrounding our posture and breathing techniques. These bad habits have become so habitual that we often think of them as being natural, when in fact we have learned them. These habits can mean that we are not using our bodies as effectively as we might and that we are actually doing ourselves physical harm by contorting our bodies into unnatural positions. When we use muscles in the wrong way, they contract and pull down. This can also lead to damaged joints and cramped internal organs. Poor posture can also cause respiratory problems.

Alexander believed that these bad habits have been picked up as a result of the stresses and strains of modern day life. Our shoulders become stiff with tension, our necks crane forward over our desks at work, our spine becomes curved from our slumped postures. When we are young babies, our posture and patterns of breathing are correct but as we grow up, we begin to learn bad habits off the adults we see around us. Alexander came to the conclusion that we have picked up so many bad habits that it has become almost impossible for us to tell what it the correct natural way to carry ourselves. Alexander's technique can help us to weed out these bad habits and replace them with a more comfortable and natural form of movement. This means that we use less energy in some activities, as our movements require less effort leaving more energy for other activities. We can relearn the correct posture and breathing that we had as children, allowing the body to rediscover a natural and comfortable stance. Realigning your posture will also improve your appearance as you will not only be slimmer in appearance but you will also give off an increased air of confidence.

The success of the Alexander Technique has continued to grow since it was first introduced in the 19th century. Thousands of people take up this technique usually to cure a specific problem such as backache, sore necks and shoulders or respiratory problems although there is evidence to support the theory that it can be beneficial to everyone whether they have a specific problem or not. The popularity of the Alexander Technique has increased particularly in recent years with conditions such as Repetitive Strain Injury emerging due to longer working hours and an increase in the number of people who worked in offices with computers. Many figures in the public eye have also been seen to advocate the Alexander Technique, which goes to show the widespread appeal of the technique. These include George Bernard Shaw, Aldous Huxley, Roald Dahl, Jeremy Irons, John Cleese, Keanu Reeves, Paul McCartney and Sting. The Alexander Technique is also taught at many prestigious centres of education including the Juillard School of Performing Arts in New York, the Royal College of Music and the Royal Academy of Dramatic Art in London and the Stratford Shakespearean Festival.

Lessons in the Alexander Technique are usually taught on a one-to-one basis although group sessions are also available. During a session, you are not required to remove clothing but it can be a good idea to wear loose baggy clothing to allow ease of movement. As with meditative sessions, lessons in the Alexander Technique are not highly energetic therefore they are suitable for those of all ages and levels of fitness. The lesson will involve the teacher observing the way that you move and carry your body. He or she will also place a hand gently on your neck, shoulders and back as you move about in order to glean more information about the way that you carry yourself. You will be asked to perform simple, everyday movements while he or she does this, such as walking around the room, sitting down and sitting up. The teacher will not only be recording the way in which you move but will also be gently manipulating your body into a more comfortable and natural posture which will release restrictive muscular tension from your body.

A lesson last from 30 to 45 minutes and people normally study the Alexander Technique for a few months before their bad habits are corrected. It is also advised that pupils attend two or three times a week at the start as it takes regular practise to overcome such deeply ingrained behavioural patterns. It is also common for ex-pupils to come back now and then for refresher courses to make sure that they do not slip back into their old bad habits.

The Alexander Technique complements meditation as the two practices share a similar goal. While the Alexander Technique does not improve your chances of reaching a higher level of consciousness, it does eliminate stress from the body, something that meditation is also said to do. Many proponents of the Alexander Technique claim that like practising meditation, practising the technique will not only improve your physical condition but will also increase you sense of mental wellbeing. In the section on factors that inhibit successful meditation, we looked at how physical discomfort can hinder our attempts to meditate. This is something which can generally be overcome with regular sessions of meditation, but by improving the way that you carry yourself through the Alexander Technique, you can overcome this more quickly and perhaps even more effectively. The Alexander Technique will relieve muscle tension and also prevent it reoccurring, which means that your meditative sessions will become more effective.

As we have seen there is much to learn on the subject of meditation and many different approaches that can be taken towards it. There are also may other alternative health therapies that you can practise in conjunction with meditation in order to make it more effective. Meditation can be taken up as a form of worship in many different religions. It also be taken up in order to improve your physical and mental health, and enhance your sense of spirituality. Whichever technique you choose, you can be sure that you will benefit from a regular practise of meditation, both physically and mentally, and your life will become enriched as a result.